W0018441

SAGE was founded in 1965 by Sara Miller McCune to support the dissemination of usable knowledge by publishing innovative and high-quality research and teaching content. Today, we publish over 900 journals, including those of more than 400 learned societies, more than 800 new books per year, and a growing range of library products including archives, data, case studies, reports, and video. SAGE remains majority-owned by our founder, and after Sara's lifetime will become owned by a charitable trust that secures our continued independence.

Los Angeles | London | New Delhi | Singapore | Washington DC | Melbourne

ADVANCE PRAISE

A timely book when the entire world is experiencing the coronavirus pandemic. Going forward, HR now has to play a significant role in creating a sustainable business model along with other stakeholders. Green HR concepts have been made easy by the authors for students and HR practitioners alike. It's a pioneering work on this new concept and my kudos to the learned authors who have made untiring efforts in research and publication of this book.

Mussarat Hussain, *Head, Leadership &*
Functional School, Maruti Suzuki

Sustainability and the concept of triple bottom line will become increasingly important in the times to come. The book is therefore topical and the authors have done a good job of outlining both the concepts relevant to this subject as well as the efforts undertaken by the various organizations.

Sidharth Balakrishna, *former Executive Director*
and Head Strategy, Essel (Zee) Group

Environment and our living conditions are changing rapidly. This has had a severe impact on our business operations and our lives in many parts of the world. This is an interesting and must-read subject for all the functions. HR is no exception. This is really a thought-provoking piece identified for HR professionals who are responsible to drive cultural changes in an organization.

Subrata Chatterjee, *Head of Human Resource,*
ArcelorMittal Design & Engg Centre (P) Ltd,
Kolkata, India

This book on Green HRM is a great road map for future leaders on how to build a sustainable organization. We can ensure a brighter future only if we take care of the environment as we grow our businesses, and this book will help leaders and managers in making the right choices.

Udit Sood, *Founder, EcoRight*

The book *Green HRM: A Climate-Conscious Route to Triple Bottom line* and, especially, the chapters on sustainability and leaders' corner have been a great read and knowledge treasure house—this will give a definite road map to industry leaders in India to rethink the way of doing business.

Soumyendra Mohan Lahiri, *Head,*
Manufacturing Excellence and EHS

Green
HRM

Green HRM

A Climate-Conscious Route to Triple Bottom Line

Soni Agrawal
Roma Puri

Los Angeles | London | New Delhi
Singapore | Washington DC | Melbourne

First published in 2021 by

SAGE Publications India Pvt. Ltd
B1/I-1 Mohan Cooperative Industrial Area
Mathura Road, New Delhi 110 044, India
www.sagepub.in

SAGE Publications Inc
2455 Teller Road
Thousand Oaks, California 91320, USA

SAGE Publications Ltd
1 Oliver's Yard, 55 City Road
London EC1Y 1SP, United Kingdom

SAGE Publications Asia-Pacific Pte Ltd
18 Cross Street #10-10/11/12
China Square Central
Singapore 048423

Published by Vivek Mehra for SAGE Publications India Pvt. Ltd. Typeset in 11.5/14.5 pt Adobe Caslon Pro by Fidus Design Pvt. Ltd, Chandigarh.

Library of Congress Control Number: 2020946311

ISBN: 978-93-5388-623-3 (PB)

SAGE Team: Namarita Kathait, Neena Ganjoo, Madhurima Thapa and Rajinder Kaur
Illustrations Credit: Raj Narayan Pratihari

To my parents and my beloved husband who always encouraged me and guided me to explore and experiment what I really believe.

Dr Soni Agrawal

To my father for being the constant in my life when everything else was changing, my friends Sumita and Subhashree for being the sounding board and always being there for me.

Dr Roma Puri

Thank you for choosing a SAGE product!
If you have any comment, observation or feedback,
I would like to personally hear from you.

Please write to me at **contactceo@sagepub.in**

Vivek Mehra, Managing Director and CEO, SAGE India.

Bulk Sales

SAGE India offers special discounts
for purchase of books in bulk.
We also make available special imprints
and excerpts from our books on demand.

For orders and enquiries, write to us at

Marketing Department
SAGE Publications India Pvt Ltd
B1/I-1, Mohan Cooperative Industrial Area
Mathura Road, Post Bag 7
New Delhi 110044, India

E-mail us at **marketing@sagepub.in**

Subscribe to our mailing list
Write to **marketing@sagepub.in**

This book is also available as an e-book.

CONTENTS

List of Abbreviations   ix

Foreword by B. L. Chandak   xiii

Preface   xv

Acknowledgements   xix

Chapter 1: People, Planet and Profit   1

Chapter 2: Cultivating Green Culture   25

Chapter 3: Green Disruptions and Sustainable
Business Models   49

Chapter 4: A Green Workplace   79

Chapter 5: Leaders' Corner   107

Chapter 6: Encouraging Green HR Practices   127

Chapter 7: Are Environmental Performance and
Green HRM Related?   141

Chapter 8: Triple Bottom Line: Leveraging Green HR
Practices   157

Chapter 9: Employee's Initiatives and Perspective   191

Chapter 10: A Greener Future   207

Glossary   239

About the Authors   245

LIST OF ABBREVIATIONS

AC	Air conditioner
ACC	Associated Cement Companies
ATF	Aviation turbine fuel
ATM	Automatic teller machines
BRR	Business responsibility report
CDM	Clean development mechanism
CDP	Committee for Development Policy
CEO	Chief executive officer
CESC	Calcutta Electric Supply Corporation
CFL	Compact fluorescent lamp
CHP	Combined heated power
CIPD	Chartered Institute of Personnel Development
CPCB	Central Pollution Control Board
CSR	Corporate social responsibility
DMT	Daily management team
EHS	Environment, health and safety
EI	Employee involvement

EIA	Environmental Impact Assessment
EM	Environment management
EMS	Environment management system
EP	Economic performance
EPR	Extended producer's responsibility
ESG	Environment, society and governance
ETP	Effluent treatment plant
EU	European Union
FIP	Focus improvement project
FY	Financial year
GHG	Greenhouse gas
GHRM	Green human resource management
GPG	Green Procurement Guideline
GRI	Global Reporting Initiative
HCL	Hindustan Computers Limited
HRM	Human resource management
HVAC	Heating, ventilating, air-conditioning
IBM	International Business Machines
INGO	International non-governmental organization
ITI	Industrial training institutes
JRD	Jehangir Ratanji Dadabhoy
KPI	Key performance indicator
KRA	Key result area
KSA	Individual knowledge, skill and ability

L&T	Larsen & Toubro
LED	Light-emitting diode
LEED	Leadership in Energy and Environment Design
LSE	London School of Economics
M&M	Mahindra & Mahindra
MNC	Multinational corporation
MT	Million tonnes
MVML	Mahindra Vehicle Manufactures Ltd
NGO	Non-governmental organization
NRDC	Natural Resources Defense Council
OECD	Organisation for Economic Co-operation and Development
PCBL	Phillips Carbon Black Limited
PM	Performance management
PPP	People, planet and profit
PTM	Parent–teacher meeting
RO	Reverse osmosis
ROCE	Return on capital employed
RWH	Rainwater harvesting
S&P	Standard & Poor's
SBM	Strategic business model
SD	Sustainable development
SDG	Sustainable Development Goals
SEBI	Securities and Exchange Board of India

SHVS	Smart hybrid vehicle from Suzuki
SIA	Social impact assessment
SRI	Solar reflective
STP	Sewage treatment plant
TBL	Triple bottom line
TCS	Tata Consultancy Services
TSR	Thermal substitution rate
TUSDAC	Trade Union Sustainable Development Advisory Committee
UN	United Nations
UNEP	United Nations Environment Program
UNFCCC	United Nations Framework Convention on Climate Change
UNIDO	United Nations Industrial Development Organization
VP	Vice president
WBSCD	World Business Council for Sustainable Development

FOREWORD

The concept of triple bottom line (TBL) is a popular concept that has been applied in the understanding of social duties among companies that are looking forward for the incorporation of non-monetary values into their businesses.

Green practices and operations, sustainability, etc., are becoming part of corporate vocabulary. The concept of sustainability and green practices has percolated to every segment of business organizations, be it operations, management, administration, human resource management (HRM), supply chain and so on.

It is important for organizations to align HRM practices with the TBL framework for wholistic success. Green human resource management (GHRM) has become one of the most critical topics in business world and sustainability. GHRM in green-oriented organizations plays a significant part in shaping the culture of sustainability in the organization. GHRM helps in creating, developing and implementing the strategy of sustainable business within the organization.

The TBL framework and reporting is no more restricted to big corporations only. It has been explained that the ultimate success of businesses ought to be measured not just by the use of the traditional financial bottom line but also by ethical and environmental factors.

I am delighted to introduce the work presented in this book. This book explores some sustainable business models that have successfully linked sustainability to strategy. The book tries to address the integration of GHRM with the TBL framework. It also gives insight into some companies that have adopted the TBL framework to evaluate their performances in a broader perspective to create better business and brand value.

Whatever the economic model, caring for and valuing people and the planet should always be central to all practices. It is only then that true will sustainability arrive.

B. L. Chandak
Executive Director, Investor Relations,
RP-Sanjiv Goenka Group

PREFACE

*The journey of a thousand miles
begins with a single step...*

This was very true for the writing of this book. The process began with the authors beginning a research project on green human resource management (GHRM). The initial idea was to write an academic book. But this changed quickly as we wanted to reach out to a critical mass of readers. While we were researching the concept, we found that there was no proper book which could act as a guide on GHRM for both practitioners and students. In fact, the idea of GHRM is still alien to a lot of people. In one of the conferences that one of us attended (this was during the preliminary days of engagement with the topic), some of the participants at the conference were pleasantly surprised that HR could have anything to do with sustainability. Till then, sustainability was the Environment Department's baby. This book is supposed to bust the myth that HRM and sustainability have no connection and also underline the important role that HRM can play in embedding sustainability in organizations.

Writing the book was a challenge as time had to be extracted from the demands of work and home, but now that the book is complete, it leaves us feeling happy and fulfilled. The journey is now over, but it has been a great learning opportunity in terms of blending theoretical concepts with practice and a dash of our imagination to create the perfect recipe for a book.

Now coming to sustainability—to sustain is to continue living on this planet with fresh air, clean water and food, and human beings need to re-establish connection with Mother Nature. Nature has already given us in abundance. With a rapid escalation of inhabitants, the subsequent increase in business has exploited a lot, and it is thus urgent to realize that we need to learn to balance the carrying capacity of Earth's supporting ecosystems.

Sustainability, *go green* initiatives and environment management (EM) are steadily becoming part of board meetings and corporate vocabulary. The giant question here is whether sustainability is the responsibility of only a handful of organizations. Is this enough on our part when we document green industry practices in sustainability reports, achievement of awards, etc.? Another imperative question is how can HR contribute to sustainability? Although in most of the cases, the standing of employees and their direct/indirect, active or passive role have not been emphasized. Also, how other organizations can take lessons from their predecessors to follow the same? Also, analysis on industry practices and benefits gained by them with the involvement of motivated employees is the prerequisite.

This book intends to answer these questions by developing a conceptual framework that links organizational factors, that is, vision and mission, leadership, organizational culture, employees' pro-environmental attitude, Green HR practices with organizational outcomes with the help of case studies of organizations.

The book begins with an explanation of sustainable development, environmentally conscious HR or Green HR and how organizations bump into mandatory sustainability requirements and where they fall short. It takes readers through sustainable business models that neatly mesh sustainability with strategy. Success stories of employees who have become agents of transformation and have transcended the organizational boundaries to promote sustainability in society add to the narrative of the book. It shares stories of how their passion resonated in their homes, workplaces and society.

This book would be of interest to students who are studying courses on sustainability, researchers who are passionate for environment conservation and senior executives and top leaders who either have begun their sustainability journey or are ready to embark on it by learning from best green practices across industries. This is an excellent source that motivates us to start with little towards the bigger aim of societal welfare at large.

ACKNOWLEDGEMENTS

The authors would like to thank Miss Namarita Kathait and the entire team of SAGE Publications for their constant support and constructive feedback. Without her continuous involvement, the book would never have taken shape. What we are most appreciative of is her role in giving a practitioner focus to this book.

On a personal note, I would like to thank and dedicate the book to my parents. They have always encouraged me and guided me to explore and experiment with what I really believe. Unconditional and constant support from my beloved husband and kids has always been my strength. They felt even more excited when they saw me working on the imperative subject of green human resource management and sustainability, which has touched me since my childhood and is a subject close to my heart. Documentation of such practices really gives me an intrinsic fulfilment.

Soni Agrawal

I would like to express my unbounded gratitude to my father for being the constant in my life when everything else was changing. Thank you, Papa, for your unconditional faith and support. Right at this moment, I am remembering my late mother, she would have been truly happy to see this book. I would also like to thank my friends Sumita and Subhashree for being the sounding board and for always being there for me. I dedicate this book to all of you.

Roma Puri

We would like to thank all the respondents who gave us time out of their busy schedules and patiently gave us insights into sustainability practices and the role of HRM in their organizations. Their comments and inputs have greatly helped in enriching the book and adding the practical dimension to it.

This work could not get completed without continuous support and encouragement from the leadership of International Management Institute, Kolkata, which had shown faith in us and supported and guided us with seed capital and resources wherever needed.

PEOPLE, PLANET AND PROFIT

> *Businesses need to go beyond the interests of their companies to the communities they serve.*
>
> **Ratan Tata**

Sustainability, greening the corporation, environment management (EM) are gradually becoming part of the corporate vocabulary. When we think about environmentally sustainable corporations, many names come to mind—Unilever, ITC Ltd, Mahindra & Mahindra (M&M), Tata Group, Ambuja Cement and many more. The big question here is whether sustainability is the responsibility of big corporations only or whether it is supposed to encompass all kinds of organizations. Should organizations see it as a solo initiative of a department to fulfil the statutory requirements or is it an investment towards the well-being of people. People, the planet and profitability, popularly known as PPP, are becoming an important consideration for organizations. Three Ps and other terms such as 'triple

Es' (economics, environment and equity) or 'triple bottom line' are frequently used to indicate a broader purpose for sustainable culture of an organization in order to optimize economic and social inputs for better environmental output over the long term. Our contention in this book is to show to the readers how sustainability needs to be embedded in the DNA of every organization, and to suggest tools and practical methodologies to help organizations don an eco-friendly avatar.

But prior to that, it is important to consider why sustainability is important at the macro level. Popular media keeps reporting stories of doomsday that the world is coming to an end. We believe that, as global citizens, we will bring this day upon ourselves as we would have consumed all the available resources on the planet. This is not just populist thinking. Stephen Hawking in one of his lectures had speculated that our planet will become uninhabitable in the next 100 years, so we need to lead space expeditions to identify other planets that could support life. These stories have relevance for all of us. Whether a doomsday would become a reality or humans would migrate to another planet—we might not live to see, but why do we bring this onto ourselves and to our future generations? Why can't we make the planet's resources abundant, secure, safe and habitable for our progenies? This reminds us of a story we were told as a child.

One day, a traveller saw a very old man sitting on the side of the road sowing seeds in a city in Kashmir. It was quite an effort for the old man, but he was at it with a single-minded concentration. On being asked what he was planting, he replied that he was planting walnut seeds. The traveller was very surprised and amused. Walnut trees take several decades to bear fruit. The old man would not even live to see the trees blossom.

The old man could read the traveller's mind. He laughed and said that he may not live to see these seeds turn into giant trees, but his grandchildren would definitely enjoy the fruit.

According to the authors, the story explains very clearly what sustainability means. Experts have defined sustainable development (SD) as follows: 'The term sustainable development was coined in *Our Common Future*. Sustainable development is the kind of development that meets the needs of the present without compromising the ability of future generations to meet their own needs.'

If we were to look closely at the sources of pollution and environmental degradation, industrialization is definitely one major pollutant. The manufacturing sector all over the world has always been blamed of polluting the environment. Carbon emissions, effluent discharges into water bodies and excessive utilization of natural resources are a reality. However, in spite of the elaborate legal framework, the implementation of the statutes has been a contentious issue and a lot of organizations have ignored the environmental side of their operations. This has been the story not only of lower-middle income and Third World countries but also of directly or indirectly high-income countries on the same path.

Hence, sustainability is everybody's responsibility. But making people, corporations and nations realize their environmental duties and responsibilities has been an arduous task. It has taken several world organizations and summits to make countries commit to environmental goals. The most recent endeavour being the macro-sustainability goals, influenced by the United Nations (UN). The Sustainable Development Goals (SDGs) are a collection of 17 global goals set by the UN General Assembly in 2015 for the year 2030. The SDGs are part of

UN Resolution 70/1. Countries are becoming signatories to important environmental causes and projects.

The report of the Committee for Development Policy (CDP) and Standard & Poor's (S&P) 500 showed that recently a number of leaders have participated, and the Climate Disclosure Leadership Index has doubled. This clearly shows that companies have started embracing transparency and are addressing the risks related to climate change.

Some of the figures that are worth mentioning here as per CDP are as follows:

- Seventy-eight per cent of respondents find business opportunities in the face of climate change. They are incorporating climate change management into long-term resilience and, in the process, creating a strategic advantage.

- Sixty-nine per cent of respondents had engaged their value chains on climate change and emissions management. This includes their workforce, suppliers, consumers, governments and communities to broaden their influence on climate change issues.

In the research of CDP, it was also devised that companies foresee opportunity of worth $2.1 trillion and market capitalization of roughly $17 trillion, which is much higher than the expected demand for electric vehicles to invest in renewables. Thus, environmental conservation, preservation and sustenance have now taken on a whole new meaning.

At present, India is focusing more on climate change and pollution control by keeping the environment, society and governance (ESG) in focus. Policies are framed in a manner that, if a company follows practices towards the safety and promotion of environment and society, there are chances of less regulatory hurdles for it. Hence, a company that is already adhering to the standards of ESG does not need to make any investments to become policy compliant. The organizations would also reap additional benefits that include increased market share and enhanced reputation among investors, customers and stakeholders.

Moreover, the emergence of green marketing, green supply chains, green management, green purchasing behaviour and green accounting are a few examples of changes happening across industries. For example, in the field of green supply chain management, organizations, especially India and China, have begun making efforts towards environmentally conscious choices in terms of designing, sourcing raw material, manufacturing and delivery of final products. These companies are given a mandate from the multinational corporations (MNCs) operating in these countries. Paradoxically, some MNCs themselves are accused of unethical environmental practices that compel them to embark on a sustainability journey (more of this later in the chapter). More the less, it is still an emerging trend, and there are very few buyers willing to pay a premium for green products.

In contrast we see the examples of some leading organizations, we find that they had started paying attention towards the environment and sustainability not only because of regulatory pressure but also to reap the benefits of better branding and a favourable global image. Customers are also gradually becoming environmentally conscious and wish to buy products and services from organizations that are environmentally responsible, and even environment conscious investors have started looking into sustainability aspects before deciding to collaborate with a partner.

If we look at the Indian perspective, recently, Indian Prime Minister Mr Narendra Modi had led the efforts to scrap plastics by 2022. In his speech on the Independence Day in 2019, he appealed to the people of the nation and government agencies to take the 'first big step' on 2 October towards the eradication of single use of plastics from India. Such effort will be a step towards conserving water, harnessing solar energy and protecting flora and fauna for a sustainable future in his address to a G7 session on the environment.

In one instance, one of the top executives from a manufacturing company interviewed for the authors' research commented that 'foreign investors and collaborators are not just interested in how profitable we are but also want to know about the sustainability initiatives of the organization before finalizing a deal. Thus, it has become an important criterion in deciding good performance as well'.

Interestingly, many organizations that have been ranked high on sustainability share a few commonalities—these organizations are quite old and experienced, their average age being 87 years; they have a lower chief executive officer (CEO)-to-average-worker pay ratio; they pay taxes timely and have higher carbon productivity. These companies generate revenues from clean goods and services, and employ more women on board. Also, these companies claim to have a link between executive pay and sustainability measures. Half of their revenue is generated from sustainable products, and their shareholders' satisfaction is higher.

Such organizations actively take steps to promote sustainability by saving energy, developing green products and retaining and motivating employees, all of which help companies to capture value through growth and return on capital employed (ROCE).

In addition, we also dive deeply into the performance of few leading companies and their sustainability efforts as how these companies behave in terms of giving back to the environment, as they had already extracted a lot from the environment. The example of creating a sustainable growth model is directed to a brand that sets an example for others. ITC is a pioneer in sustainability initiatives, contributing to India's economic, social and environmental growth in a commendable manner. ITC has always followed the motto of 'Let's Put India First' and has made serving national priorities its goal. ITC is the first company in India to voluntarily apply for corporate governance rating. ITC has also achieved many accolades, such as carbon positive for 9 successive years, water positive for 12 consecutive years and solid waste recycling positive for the past 7 years. The sustainability initiatives of ITC will be discussed in more detail later in the chapter.

There are instances in which companies had to develop a sustainability strategy as a reaction to pressure from the local government or the community.

SPICEJET REDUCED CARBON FOOTPRINTS

Some of the stories that were widely reported in the media on sustainability include the stories of SpiceJet. The airlines industry reels under pressure of ever-escalating prices of aviation turbine fuel (ATF), which is a serious cause for undermining the profitability of airlines. The different commercial liners keep exploring ways to save on the usage of ATF. SpiceJet not only showed a way to cut ATF costs but also made it more environmentally friendly. In 2018, it flew its test flight from Dehradun to Delhi using a combination of ATF and biojet fuel manufactured in its Jatropha Plant in Dehradun. The benefits of biojet fuel are reduced carbon emissions and increased fuel efficiency. Thus, they could get a sustainable solution while solving their commercial problem.

COCA-COLA: FROM POLLUTER TO SAVER

The plant of Coca-Cola in Rajasthan is a case in point. Coke was accused of depleting the underground water levels that affected farming in areas near Jaipur after the entry of MNCs into the region. In another instance, Coca-Cola was forced to temporarily shut down one of its plants near Varanasi, Uttar Pradesh, for extracting ground-level waters beyond legal limits and releasing toxic effluents into water. In fact, the detection of traces of pesticide in Pepsi and Coke brought further disrepute to Coca-Cola and its competitor, where customers began boycotting their products. These events triggered a series of environment-friendly initiatives from Coca-Cola in which it stressed its role as a water steward. It initiated a number of water replenishment projects, and the targets for replenishment went way above the legal limits. Coca-Cola created a replenishment potential of around 1,900 per cent of the water used (19 times the water used by the plant) by its Kaladera plant as of December 2015—'a potential of 6.8 billion litres of water replenishment has been created, impacting the lives of over 6 Lakh people from more than 500 villages in India.' As part of its community development efforts, Coca-Cola India initiated the Project Unnati, which was meant to source 95 per cent ingredients used in the manufacturing process locally from the local farmer community, and it intended to enhance the scope of the project by involving more than 4 lakh farmers by 2023. It intends to reduce its carbon footprint by reducing carbon dioxide emissions by 25 per cent that are part of its operations by by 2020.[1]

Although we see organizations embed sustainability in their vision and mission statements, and leaders too ensure, how they would like their organizations to become sustainable, but the litmus test of sustainability would be when sustainability gets ingrained in employee behaviour. This would only be possible when employees understand the importance of sustainability and adopt pro-environmental or sustainability-oriented behaviour in their day today life as well. In the absence of employee involvement (EI), sustainability initiatives can never

---

[1] https://www.coca-colaindia.com/

be successful and organizations experience lapses that hurt their reputation and highlight a dichotomy between what is promised and what actually gets done.

MAHINDRA & MAHINDRA SAVES BRAND IMAGE WITH SUSTAINABILITY

Let us take the case of M&M. It is a very well-respected company that has a number of SD projects. M&M has also been ranked among the most sustainable companies. Very recently, M&M was caught on the wrong foot. A picture of the M&M Board meeting was shared on twitter. One of the twitter users pointed out the use of disposable plastic bottles in the Board meeting of M&M. This prompted Mr Mahindra to take ownership and banish plastic bottles from meetings and replace them with environment-friendly alternatives.

This simple narrative points out how the organizers of the meeting had not thought about the environmental implications of their actions (using plastic bottles in the meeting) when the company is actively promoting the environment and sustainability, and this may be true for employees across organizations as well who are neither aware of nor committed to the environmental cause. Hence, EI becomes important for organizations on their sustainability journey.

EVOLUTION OF HR AS GREEN HR

Leading organizations that are concerned for the environment and sustainability and are active in environmental conservation get positive outcomes in terms of better performance. To have an effective EM, the support of employees has been found to be very critical. HR plays a crucial role in generating a sustainable competitive advantage. It is believed that well-crafted HR policies and practices are very important for reinforcing and sustaining employee actions in line with organizational capabilities, culture, group-level job competencies, norms and individual knowledge, skill and abilities (KSAs), and opportunities. This has led to the emergence of a new concept named as green human resource management (GHRM). It can be understood to be the human aspect of EM.

The involvement of HR can either be direct or indirect. It can be in the form of recruiting, training or rewarding employees for maintaining or augmenting green workplace behaviour in the organization.

Several mechanisms may be used to make human resource management (HRM) environment oriented. In fact, there can be a green orientation throughout the life cycle of an employee. The recruitment strategy of the company needs to be influenced with the basic motive of selecting employees who have a positive concern towards the environment. It is suggested that the mention of environmental performance in vacancy notices improves the chances of attracting and recruiting competent employees. Attracting environmentally aware talent might be facilitated by proactive branding of the organization as a high-quality 'green employer of choice'. After selecting candidates for posts, companies can provide necessary basic information about the corporate EM policies, systems and practices. New recruits need to be inducted into the corporate's environment culture. Also, they need to be taught how to integrate EM in their routine work.

The existing employees are provided training to reinforce positive management efforts such as recycling and waste management, supporting flexible schedules & telecommuting, and reducing long-distance business travel. Increasing environmental awareness among the workforce by organizing seminars and workshops at the organizational level is also vital to accomplish effective environmental performance. It is important to disseminate environmental information to induce behavioural change among managers and non-managerial employees. Well-trained and environmentally aware front-line employees are preferably placed for identifying and reducing waste as they are closely working with it. Some companies adhere to teamwork as well as cross-functional teams for successfully managing environmental issues of the company. Job narratives and specifications may comprise environmental, social, personal and technical requirements of organizations.

Green performance management (PM) and compensation practices guide employees to align their behaviours with the environmental objectives of the organization. Key performance indicators (KPIs) related to green behaviour should be accessible to all the employees at all levels. Also, this should be a part of the company's culture and regular employee conversation related to green matters. Managers shall set green targets, goals and responsibilities for their sections, divisions or departments, which shall be assessed later through some metrics such as the number of green incidents, moreover, the use of environmental responsibility and the successful communication of environmental policy must be within the scope of their operations. Reward and recognition systems can also be instituted to encourage employee green behaviour. EI and participation in green suggestion schemes and problem-solving circles helps in many ways. It may include creating employees as how they can practise green behaviour. This includes facilitation with a helpline number addressing queries, schemes and support from management and union, etc. Also, employees need to be motivated to use green forms of transport and related actions. A green whistle-blowing helpline can also be initiated to continuously monitor the environment management system (EMS) at the shop floor level as well.

THE SUSTAINABILITY PIONEERS

According to the Futurescape 2018, the companies that are honoured as most promising of green India are Tata Chemicals Ltd (TCL), M&M, ITC, Ambuja Cement Ltd, Tata Motors, Tata Power Company Ltd, Infosys, Bharat Petroleum Corporation Ltd, Hindustan Zinc and Indian Oil Corporation Ltd. These companies have framed their investments in such a manner that their business interests are achieved in a scalable manner.

The company that is highly admired and received a very high score in the race of sustainability globally is TCL. TCL had implemented a number of schemes to save energy across its plants, including the commissioning of a solar photovoltaic plant. The reason behind this was to control greenhouse gas (GHG) emissions in order to harness non-polluting renewable energy resources. TCL is world's second largest producer of soda ash. The company has a global manufacturing presence and has always kept safety under due consideration while implementing various features such as Target Zero Harm programme, Suraksha Jyoti at Mithapur, Process Safety Management at Babrala, Srestho at Haldia, RAMP (long-term asset management plan) at TCNA and Safety Amnesty at TCE. It had introduced plant inspection rounds at Mithapur and Haldia, and rail safety management at TCM. Ergonomic surveys were also conducted from time to time towards ensuring healthy workplace lighting and safe working postures. TCL Babrala is one of the lowest energy-consuming units among fertilizer units and the most energy-efficient unit in India. It is also working to improve its energy management by implementing ISO 50001 to monitor and manage energy use. TCL's soda ash plant is one of the lowest carbon emitters in the European Union (EU). The company understands that minimization of waste is beneficial to both the economy and the environment.

The company ensures that all sites must strictly enforce on-site segregation of waste so that all hazardous and non-hazardous waste can be sold to authorized and registered dealers and all organic waste is composted. TCL is dedicated to safety and its Zero Harm target resonates through the company, right from senior management all the way to on-ground employees.

Another company which is appreciated on it sustainability part is M&M and sustainable business model is under its 'rise' philosophy. You cannot rise if you take more from the community than you put back. It is imperative for us to protect the flora and fauna around us', said CMD Anand Mahindra, M&M. In 2016, M&M has become the first Indian company to set an internal carbon price (US$10 per tonne of carbon emitted). The move was in line with its business commitment for reducing its GHG emissions. Over the last two years, the total water consumption has come down by almost 134,696 m. M&M had won the Indo-German Chamber of Commerce Award 2017 for 'best sustainable business practices'.

Moreover, M&M comes forward towards helping employees and connect them with company's sustainable practices. Not only M&M is leading in sustainability initiatives but it is also achieving improved economic performance (EP). In 2017, M&M crossed global sales of 1 million vehicles and tractors (520,286 vehicles and 302,082 tractors), a growth of 10.8 per cent in the automotive sector and 21.5 per cent in the farm equipment sector over the previous year. M&M and Mahindra Vehicle Manufactures Ltd (MVML) recorded an increase of 15 per cent in net sales and operating income at ₹475.77 billion in 2017 as against ₹413.78 billion in the previous year. Beroz Gazdar, senior vice president (VP) group sustainability, orated that the strategy for charting a sustainability course at M&M is quite simple. It influences a number of business verticals to appreciate this as an emerging business model that can be leveraged later. About half of M&M's stakeholders, including its supply chain, are aligned to the group's sustainability vision. Employee participation in the volunteering programme has increased significantly over the years. Gazdar uses a simple argument.

> If we're talking about water conservation in our factories, I simply point out that without water, there would be no operations. No water, no work. They immediately understand why not saving water, or trying to improve the water table around our plants, can be a business risk.

Breaking the myth that only men can work in core manufacturing due to the use of heavy machinery, M&M hired a number of women on the shop floor in the automotive, steel and intertrade sectors. At a time when women employees working on the shop floor was not common, they successfully challenged the mindset and currently have more than 100 women employees in manufacturing. M&M is the pioneer of electric vehicles and integrated mobility solutions in India. The launch of the e-Alfa Mini is yet another step towards providing an emission-free, green mode of safe intercity transportation in the country.

Another company that is appreciated on sustainability ground is Ambuja Cement Ltd. Their commitment towards sustainability is reflected in two plants that accomplished 'zero harm' and the seven sites that recorded 'zero lost time injury' and achieved a 34 per cent reduction in total on-site injuries, a 31 per cent reduction in total injury frequency rate and a 37 per cent in lost time injury frequency rate. Moreover, Ambuja is the pioneer in innovating towards meeting the needs of its customers in a more environmentally favourable manner. New products and solutions, such as Ambuja Compocem (composite cement), Ambuja Cool Walls (environment-friendly blocks), Ambuja Modular Curing Solution (a water-saving green alternative for curing), rooftop rainwater harvesting (RWH) system (for water conservation and storage) and Ambuja Pura Sand (manufactured sand for plastering) are worth noting. These products and solutions not only fulfil important customer needs but also significantly conserve natural resources. This company is one of the most carbon-efficient cement companies in India. The carbon emissions of the company is reduced to 529.6 kg CO_2/tonne of cement (31.4% lower as compared to our 1990 baseline) and also to a reduced clinker-to-cement ratio, which indicates less consumption per tonne of product that was done by using alternative fuels, raw materials and improving efficiency in our processes. The company provides waste management solutions under the brand Geocycle. In 2018, the company fed 0.3 million tonnes (MT) of waste into the kilns as alternative fuels and attained a thermal substitution rate of 5.6 per cent, higher by 33 per cent over the previous year, and also co-processed whopping 69,000 tonnes of plastic waste in kilns—twice the total plastic used in cement bags, thus offsetting plastic use. Moreover, about 8 MT of waste derived from raw materials such as fly ash and slag generated by power stations and steel plants were used, thus bringing down clinker factor to as low as 65 per cent in the production of low-carbon pozzolana cement and composite cement. As a result, a considerable amount of fossil fuel and natural raw materials were saved in production process. Without a doubt, Ambuja Cement is still on the journey to realize the vision as the most sustainable cement company in India and globally. Moreover, the EP of the company is also on the growth trajectory. Sales increased by 7.1 per cent over the last year and net profit increased by 18 per cent in financial year (FY) 2018.

Efforts taken by ITC towards the environment and sustainability need to be mentioned here. In the past few years, the company had spent considerable money on developing renewable energy infrastructure. And now, 60 per cent of its total requirement is met with renewable energy, which includes sources such as wind and solar power. Also, if we talk about waste management, over 99 per cent of solid waste is either recycled or reused. As far as EP is concerned, ITC in 2018 realized a 6 per cent increase in gross sales and profit before interest and tax, which was increased by 7 per cent over the last year. This is indeed remarkable, considering the huge manufacturing base and hotels of the company. In addition, many of ITC's buildings have achieved the highest levels of LEED certification, and the few are even 'Platinum certified'. ITC Hotels have pioneered the concept of 'responsible luxury', becoming the greenest luxury hotel chain in the world. The transformational journey of ITC has been enriched with its success in creating large-scale societal value.

Here, the authors had taken a deep dive for understanding the environment and sustainability in ITC. In ITC, for achieving success in green initiatives at an organizational level, support of HR is considered crucial. It includes all the stakeholders in practice. Thus, it becomes important in the organization to understand and identify stakeholders who are directly or indirectly influenced by the business activities as well as those who directly or indirectly influence the business activities. The process of identifying such stakeholders is guided by attributes such as dependency, responsibility, immediacy and influence. In addition, the company also conducts the need assessment surveys as part of stakeholder engagement along with engaging stakeholders such as government, developing agencies, research organization and communities on various platforms. To attract and retain the best talent, the culture of 'building winning businesses', 'building business leaders' and 'creating value for India' is promoted. The process of creating a shared mindset across organizations for ensuring that employees are inspired, engaged and aligned to the company's mission, vision, values and strategic agenda is always reinforced. Towards building a talent pipeline across all levels, training and development support is also encouraged. Along with that, harmonious employee relations are built for enabling smooth functioning and productivity enhancement. Also, the importance of diverse workforce and nurturing specialism to meet the requirements is also seen in a positive manner.

For achieving best performance from their highly motivated team is not a challenge for ITC, as ITC believes in aligning the compensation structure with the performance at the company, business and individual levels, including the adequate weightage to the variable pay component. Smooth and good employee relations are ensured with having an empathetic approach towards employees. Without compromising on the increase of cost in a product line, flexible work systems are provided to employees as needed.

Do you know why the *United Nations* Framework Convention on Climate Change (UNFCCC) has significant value today?

Read more at https://unfccc.int/

THE SUSTAINABILITY IMPERATIVE

The question arises here if the benefits of environmental and sustainability initiatives are so obvious, why aren't more companies adopting the same? Can we infer that sustainability is going to be an emerging mega-trend in the coming years? Over the past 10 years, environment-related issues have steadily influenced the capacity of the businesses for creating values for customers, shareholders and other stakeholders. The rise of new world powers, notably China and India, has intensified competition for natural resources (especially oil) and added a geopolitical dimension to sustainability. 'Externalities' such as carbon dioxide emissions and water usage are quickly becoming material—meaning that investors consider them central to a firm's performance, and stakeholders expect companies to share information about them.

These forces are magnified by escalating public and governmental concern about climate change, industrial pollution, food safety and natural resource depletion, among other issues. Consumers in many countries are demanding sustainable products. Globally, governments are interceding with unprecedented levels of new regulations towards better control on environmental pollution. Another dimension is that even top management of leading companies globally are showing concerns and putting efforts towards making their operations sustainable and developing 'green' products. They demand such processes to be followed by their vendors as well. Many of the small- and medium-sized enterprises find themselves in a disadvantageous position vis-à-vis their rivals.

On the contrary, many companies in lower-middle income and Third World countries do not face the pressure in the similar manner. Suppliers hesitate to provide green products or use the green supply chain. They are not transparent towards sustainable manufacturing, as it demands new improved equipment and processes, which requires extra investment in their existing technology. The choice is between green products and services and the additional costs that are to be incurred. An additional challenge arises when customers are unwilling to pay more for eco-friendly products and services. 'Most companies still have a long way to go in terms of properly assessing climate risk,' said Nicolette Bartlett, CDP's Director of Climate Change.

DISCUSSION ON ALTERNATIVES

One option may be that policy experts and environmental activists need to remain tough with regulation. The argument here is that voluntary action is not enough for the bigger cause that we have now. Existing regulatory requirements, such as the perform, achieve, trade and renewable energy certificate schemes and future regulatory pressures in line with India are needed. At the same time, practical aspects need to be considered before having tough regulations. For example, the commitment under the Nationally Determined Contributions and the Paris Agreement (December 2015) on the UNFCCC is increasing competition for the usage of biomass, but the lack of viable alternatives for fossil fuels for meeting the thermal energy requirements is an issue here. Some other burning concerns include risks involved in off-site renewable energy investments, weak infrastructure linkages, restriction on interstate wheeling/banking of electricity, open access, etc.

But, despite the initial challenges, we need to keep on moving with small steps; for example, success stories of some of the companies that have converted themselves green can also be quoted to mobilize and create interests among existing players. The example can be quoted here of GE, where in 2005 CEO Jeff Immelt decided that the company would focus on tackling environmental issues. Since then, every GE business has tried to move up on the sustainability ladder, which has helped the conglomerate take the lead in several industries. Some other alternatives towards the softer side can also be considered, which include educating and mobilizing consumers, so that they demand sustainable and green products and services.

Although both legislation and education are necessary, they may not be able to solve the problem quickly or completely at least.

Here, the support of HR can also be cherished, where emphasis can be given towards recruiting and retaining the right kind of people. It can be inferred here that there is now an increasing trend, especially in high-income countries, with regard to social responsibility and environmental commitment. Companies give due emphasis to sustainability mindset as a quality in the prospective employees for being selected. Sustainability can be given due importance from day one and all stakeholders need to be involved to follow the mission of the organization. Also, to achieve such an initiative, the company will need a workforce that appreciates sustainability for collectively developing a low-carbon economy.

SUGGESTED READINGS

Giannarakis, G., Konteos, G., Sariannidis, N., & Chaitidis, G. (2017). The relation between voluntary carbon disclosure and environmental performance: The case of S&P 500. *International Journal of Law and Management*, *59*(6), 784–803. https://doi.org/10.1108/

Harvey, G., Williams, K., & Probert, J. (2013). Greening the airline pilot: HRM and the green performance of airlines in the UK. *The International Journal of Human Resource Management*, *24*(1), 152–166.

Jabbour, C. J. C., Santos, F. C. A., & Nagano, M. S. (2010). Contributions of HRM throughout the stages of environmental management: Methodological triangulation applied to companies in Brazil. *The International Journal of Human Resource Management*, *21*(7), 1049–1089.

Nidumolu, R., Prahalad, C. K., & Rangaswami, M. R. (2009). Why sustainability is now the key driver of innovation. *Harvard Business Review, 87*(9), 56–64.

Renwick, D. W. S., Redman, T., & Maguire, S. (2008). *Green HRM: A review, process model, and research agenda* (Working Paper No. 2008.01). University of Sheffield. https://pdfs.semantic scholar.org/7139/feee5b4acf5f53b97466f5f9c6881e92c4a8. pdf?_ga=2.241761730.1515554351.1597898372-1146323717. 1597898372

Renwick, D. W. S., Redman, T., & Maguire, S. (2013). Green human resource management: A review, and research agenda. *International Journal of Management Review, 15*(1), 1–14.

https://www.financialexpress.com/industry/your-money-the-advantages-of-being-esg-compliant/1609500/

https://www.itcportal.com/sustainability/index.aspx

https://www.thehindubusinessline.com/economy/global-companies-see-climate-change-hitting-their-bottom-lines-in-next-5-years/article27433152.ece#

//economictimes.indiatimes.com/articleshow/70255710.cms? utm_source=contentofinterest&utm_medium=text&utm_ campaign=cppst

//economictimes.indiatimes.com/articleshow/70721687. cms?utm_source=contentofinterest&utm_medium=text&utm_ campaign=cppst

//economictimes.indiatimes.com/articleshow/45372587. cms?utm_source=contentofinterest&utm_medium=text&utm_ campaign=cppst

https://www.futurescape.in/responsible-business-rankings/

https://futurism.com/stephen-hawking-humanity-only-has-100-years-left-on-earth-before-doomsday

https://science.slashdot.org/story/17/06/22/1718259/stephen-hawking-says-he-is-convinced-that-humans-need-to-leave-earth

https://krmangalam.edu.in/blog/sustainable-development-need-hour/

https://www.indiatimes.com/news/india/after-swachh-bharat-abhiyan-india-will-take-pledge-to-become-plastic-free-on-gandhi-jayanti-374587.html

https://www.hindustantimes.com/india-news/at-g7-summit-pm-modi-highlights-india-s-large-scale-efforts-towards-eliminating-single-use-plastic/story-E1pn8U2DDgNVcu GvwlyDeI.html

CULTIVATING GREEN CULTURE

Global warming is a universal issue, and the solution to the problem can also come from us only. The way the natural resources are extracted and consumed from the earth, it is going to be very difficult to replenish them in a timely manner. It is often discussed in various forums that, for generating the resources we spend in one year, the earth takes around 1.5 years to regenerate. Hence, it can be assumed that there will be a requirement of the capacity of almost two Earths by 2030 to keep pace with present natural resource consumption, and that almost three planets will be required by 2050. For the purpose of reducing carbon emissions globally, the support and guidance of all stakeholders are necessary.

Some countries have already started showing interest towards the social cause. For example, when the UK government, with the support of the British Carbon Trust, had conducted a survey in 2001 for assessing the impact of the policy on 'reducing the level of carbon emissions', it was found that 75 per cent of the sample of employees agreed that it is an important issue and welcomed the approach of the government. In another survey on HR professionals in 2007, it was found that

47 per cent of them stated that they would choose working for firms that have a strong green perspective. It is understood that the pro-environmental perspective needs increased employee awareness, knowledge and skills in both processes and material, and this requires an integrated training in EM for creating an emotional involvement for environmental concerns. It is seen that in Britain, the Trades Union Congress has established its own body on sustainability, the Trade Union Sustainable Development Advisory Committee (TUSDAC), to develop employee training and skills in energy-efficient technologies. Although TUSDAC sometimes pointed out that union representatives face the issues of getting paid time off to attend green development courses, the number of unions has increased, including environmental issues in their activist training. The survey conducted by Chartered Institute of Personnel Development (CIPD)/KPMG reported that 42 per cent of UK organizations educate and train employees in business practices that are environment friendly and train employees for acknowledging the threats that climate change may pose on firms.

In India, the Natural Resources Defense Council (NRDC) took steps towards building a low carbon-based sustainable economy in 2009. NRDC, with its partners, works on projects that can increase building efficiency, prepare policies for public health on climate changes, strengthen governance towards environment protection and enhance India and US cooperation on climate change.

Moreover, in another survey on two countries, such as the UK and Japan, on 53 companies combined, it was found that employees prefer working in companies that are sensible towards the environment, and that it is 'easier to hire high quality employees if a firm had a better environmental reputation'. On the other hand, environmentally sensitive companies do prefer to recruit employees who are motivated and have knowledge about EM. In the USA, during the Obama administration, almost £300 m were spent on training for green jobs.

The Indian Environmental Society for the safeguarding of the Himalayas focuses on understanding the Himalayan ecosystem. The society is instrumental in developing policy measures to sustain this with the help of communities around. Another effort by the Indian government was taken with the help of National Action Plan on Climate Change in 2008. The society identified eight core sectors that need the utmost attention. Here, control on GHG emission is given the utmost importance.

Thus, it can be inferred that people have started to think and to present their values consistently both from the heart and from the head. The current requirement is towards developing long-term, meaningful relationships and self-discipline for attaining effective results. In the real sense, first we need to have the ability to believe in ourselves that we can achieve it. Values are the essential characteristics that both employees and organizations uphold and operate at multiple levels (societal, organizational and personal) and thus play a fundamental role in shaping the organization's culture with regard to a shift towards greater sustainability.

An approach towards more sustainable organization needs a commitment beyond 'recycling'. This can be an issue of education, but it also comprises developing an understanding of how to enact good intentions. This can also cover exploring areas of good practice as well as perceived and actual barriers. In short, what makes it possible for individuals and organizations to see a linkage between the information they have and what they need to do in practice and their behaviour. There are organizations that see sustainability as a key to the way they do business, because they simply believe in 'the right thing to do'. Although for others, it might be in terms of raised public expectations.

Implementing green practices throughout the organization is a challenging task, and here the role of human resource managers becomes crucial. It is appreciated that the stakeholder approach to sustainability needs to be intimated through an open-system structure that identifies the correlation and interaction of stakeholders, organizational systems and sub-systems, that is, the social systems and the environment in which they operate.

Besides, there are two major stakeholders that can influence an organization's adoption decisions: (a) external stakeholders and (b) internal stakeholders. Allying the two categories, external stakeholders, such as customers and regulators, are viewed as a firm's most influential stakeholders.

External stakeholders, especially government or industry, may constrain organizations in adopting green practices, for example, the carbon emissions trading scheme in Australia influenced the top management to adopt a green approach in their business. Customers may also request companies to apply a certain environmental certification to their products, or the top management may be obliged to espouse green operations either by averting a penalty or by preserving their market share or profitability.

Internal stakeholders, such as HR management teams, middle managers or employees, may also be considered as influential stakeholders. Their expectations can also encourage a firm to espouse green HR initiatives in a bid to attract employees. Besides, there is growing evidence that the career choices of graduates who prefer working in an organization that values sustainability are increasing, and thus recruitment for employees is also determined by the sustainability agenda of employers consequently. Moreover, Green HR initiatives can be viewed as radical changes within an organization that require sufficient time and resources to be formulated into practice.

It is seen that organizational enthusiasm may be perceived as operational readiness, financial readiness, personnel readiness, technical readiness as well as knowledge readiness. HR managers need to magnetize and motivate their employees towards green practices. Organizations concerned for the environment and sustainability are not only active towards environmental sustainability but are also perceiving positive outcomes, such as higher profitability, better financial performance and higher stock prices. In contrast, the survey conducted by the Society for Human Resource Management demonstrated that only 22 per cent of organizations usually adopt green HR initiatives, and 50 per cent of firms have no plans at all to adopt them.

The GHRM concept is relatively new and emerging. Moreover, it is seen that major MNCs have started acquiring GHRM practices in the form of employer branding. The HR of these companies have already started improvising their selection allurement for an increasingly environmental conscious younger generation. Job seekers are assessed not only on their technical and behavioural skills but also on how much they give values to environmental and sustainability-related values of the organization. Thus, the organization's prestigious image and esteemed values play a prominent role in the recruitment endeavour.

Do you know about Tata Consultancy Services' (TCS) community initiative and impact?

Read more at https://www.tcs.com/community-initiatives-and-impact

GREEN LEADERSHIP

For the successful implementation of the vision, mission and values of the organization, the role of leader becomes very vital. Employees look up to them for guidance and motivation. It is seen that the participation of senior management is considered essential as they can create and foster conditions through their endorsement. Consequently, it is possible that an organization's senior management has an ecological world view and is aware of the firm's environmental impact. It is notable that attitude plays a key role in one's behaviour pertaining to individuals as well as to organizations.

A leader who is passionate for sustainability and values diversity plays an important role here. It is he who theatres the role of 'employee champion' and is thus instrumental in utilizing professional expertise for prompt services towards supervising key instruments of organizational change.

Another important aspect is recruiting employees with green attitudes and experience. It is also seen that when senior management perceives that their organization has sufficient resources for executing green HR activities, they tend to adopt them more. Due to the absence of insufficient resources, senior management may have great difficulty in offering or imposing green policies and practices.

When we talk about leadership, the eco-centric values of leaders and flexibility in terms of implementing policies play an important role as found while interviewing 73 Canadian and US leaders (of for-profit and non-profit product and service organizations). Moreover, integrity and commitment towards building enduring organizations, and having a profound desire for building the image of their company towards meeting the needs of all stakeholders who value the planet and society at large, play an important role.

Leadership is one of the essential elements of organizational effectiveness. Although the development of leadership capability is the foremost debate for evolving business strategies for ecological sustainability, leadership is seen to be crucial for organizations that accept a positive perspective on sustainability. Although leadership is not constricted to specified roles within a department of the organization, rather it exhibits its role throughout the process of building the organization sustainable and green.

It is seen in the research findings from 186 US firms on the *Forbes* list that there is a strong relationship between CEO compensation (total compensation and salary) and the firm's environmental reputation, but CEOs are not inevitably rewarded for their firm's EM record, moreover, nor are they invigorated towards doing so by the structure of such compensation systems. In one of the study of 207 US firms from the S&P 500, it was revealed that EM initiatives are successful only in those firms which have a direct linkage between environmental performance and executive contracts. Thus, it is the confirmation of the linkage between environmental performance and compensation to the CEO.

In order to make GHRM work, it is very important that both employers and employees must understand the importance and value of the process in day-today function. Top management must also know the value of communicating externally about the successes as well as the challenges of their organization.

HR POLICIES AND PRACTICES

It is seen that pro-environmental perspective needs increased employee awareness, knowledge and skills in both processes and practices, thus requiring integrated training on EM for creating emotional involvement in environmental concerns.

Here, it is seen that HRM's stance as the key interface with the management and employees of the organization lends itself to proceed a leadership role in relation to issues that need innovative interventions. It also provides HRM the opportunity to indicate their 'strategic' contribution to wider organizational values, rather than constantly competing on proving their financial credentials.

GHRM denotes the social as well as human outcomes that contribute to the continuation of the organization in the long run. GHRM is the application of HRM policies for encouraging the sustainable use of resources within the organization and for comprehensively upgrading the practice of environmental sustainability. It is seen that HRM activities enhance positive environmental results. A well environmentally practised organization must accentuate the practices in all key HR functions, such as developing job descriptions, having environment-related key factors, recruitment and selection practices, training activities, performance evaluations parameters, including environment-related key indicators, feedback mechanism, suggestion schemes, and rewarding and recognizing employees, with great efforts towards the environment and management.

In a survey and interview with 156 plant-level employees among 31 lean automobile assembly plants in North America and Japan, it was found that HR practices encourage higher levels of environmental training and are very much needed for the development of skills required for waste reduction.

An MNC based in India had planned an initiative in partnership with Exnora International, an environmental non-governmental organization (NGO) for generating income of individuals. In this approach, household garbage was collected and, after processing and recycling, biodegradable waste was converted into organic manure. Moreover, a wider community-awareness program on environment and how to reduce waste or how to protect the environment in a better manner were also practised.

GHRM is promptly responsible for creating green workforce that understands, appreciates and practises green initiatives and preserves its green objectives all throughout the HRM process of recruiting, hiring, training, compensating, developing and advancing the firms' human capital. It denotes to the policies, practices and systems that make employees of the organization green for the welfare of individuals, society, the natural environment and business.

It is seen that HR policies and practices have changed due to global environmental variability. These policies and practices are the key elements for successful EM. HR policies can definitely play an important role at the national level in depleting GHG emissions (e.g., a step may be by carpooling or recycling programmes).

Thus, the policies and practices as shared by HR managers are as follows: before going for recruitment, there is a need to develop job descriptions and personnel specifications that accentuate the environmental aspects of the job. Thereafter, while conducting interview, some protocols must be followed, which would be able to evaluate the applicant's environmental knowledge, values and beliefs.

Also, communication of such attributes needs to be disseminated all over and needs to be aligned with the practices followed in all HR functions. Then only candidates will be able to see such attributes in practice that will ultimately enhance the image and reputation of the organization.

Moreover, the support of technology can be used by going paperless. HR can start this quite early with new employees by inducting them with the use of online portals and folders to archive employee documentation such as offer letters, credentials, CVs or recommendation letters. Besides, when newcomers first arrive at the office, the induction programmes should be sketched in such a way as to ease the unification of these new employees with the company's traditions of green consciousness. Besides portraying the company, its history, culture, departments and others, these programmes should also accentuate the company's concerns with regard to environmental issues and the green actions being developed both inside the company (in offices or in other facilities) and with outside stakeholders.

PM is another way in which green PM systems can be successfully initiated in order to develop performance indicators for each area of environmental risk. Green performance appraisals comprise topics such as environmental incidents, the use of environmental responsibilities and the communication of environmental concerns and policies. It is realized that it is important for the successful implementation of these policies. There needs to be an alignment between strategic approaches towards reward management. This can be defined as aligning pay practices and corporate objectives. There are some examples for organizations that are discussed in detail in later chapters as how these companies developed systems to streamline their strategic policies that were aligned with pay incentives to EM, especially for senior managers.

Recognition-based rewards for staff in EM (such as company-wide public recognition) can be implemented in large MNCs and may be offered at different levels; for example, some awards can be announced annually on the basis of contributions to individuals, teams or divisional contributions for reducing waste. Company-wide team excellence awards and in other non-traditional forms, such as giving employees opportunities to attend green events/rallies, may also be promoted. Here, the example of Indian conglomerate TCS seems appropriate to mention, which runs a programme called 'GEM' to recognize the efforts by its employees towards social and environment causes. Here, instant recognition and sometimes just simple rewards are given for motivating employees. It also helps the company in retaining the talent.

Other such innovative non-pecuniary rewards for employees' EM actions include paid vacations, time offs and gift certificates. It is seen that environmental rewards and recognition (such as daily praise and company awards) have a significant impact on employees' willingness to implement eco-initiatives. Such initiatives are able to produce an open style of communication that encourages employees to discuss their environmental ideas 'in an honest and unrestricted manner'. In Britain, some examples of company practices include the use of a 'carbon credit card' and cash incentives for staff to snap up hybrid cars, incentive schemes, rewarding good attendance/performance with a 'green benefit card', enabling staff purchases of green products and annual awards dinners to recognize exemplary behaviour in EM. Examples of providing financial incentives for EM reward strategies in a UK firm include, for example, tax incentives and exemptions to promote the loaning of bicycles to employees and the use of a less polluting car fleet.

It is seen that the EI or wider employee participation in EM predicts the success of an inventiveness taken by an organization, rather than restricting the involvement to managers and specialists. Restricted approach is often found as negative for successful outcomes. A Belgian study on high-level polluters (as measured by environmental taxes paid) also found a significant relationship between firms that identify themselves as practising environmental leadership and attaching high importance to their employee stakeholders. For instance, low-carbon champions, work-based recycling schemes, establishing specific green/environmental action teams to discuss how to involve staff in helping firms become more environmental friendly, and encouraging employees to use tele/videoconferencing, car sharing and home-working are all recent developments directed towards engaging employees in environmental initiatives. Development of tacit knowledge is particularly found useful in identifying sources of pollution, managing emergency situations and developing preventive solutions.

Some of the day-to-day green practices followed in the organization include the use of less paper or the use of paper only when it is really necessary, encouraging printing, in case needed on both sides, providing training programmes or information sessions to employees on green practices, etc. Examples of how employee training on EM is vital in order to inculcate core EM skills in employees include how to collect relevant waste data or develop training modules that stress on 'eco-literacy' and environmental protection. It is assumed that well-trained and environmentally aware employees are only able to minimize the usage and reduce waste as they are adjacent to it.

Some of the examples as shared by companies for reducing carbon emissions include the following: the use of car sharing, taking benefit of free or discounted transportation passes and hybrid/electric cars offered by the company, walking or cycling to work, working from home once or twice a week. Besides this, for reducing waste, the use of porcelain mugs and glasses for tea and coffee is promoted. The approach of promoting the 3Rs (reduce, reuse and recycle) using electronic archives and electronic signatures is some of the initiatives to eschew the wastage of paper.

Do you know about India's Green NGO Exnora International?
Read more at https://en.wikipedia.org/wiki/Exnora_International

TIPS TOWARDS GOING GREEN

Importance of Green Team

It is sure that the organization has employees who already make green choices at home, are well aware of environmental topics and are enthusiastic about greening the job site. It might be useful for the organization to engage such employees by assigning them to a committee to oversee green initiatives. The green team can execute recycling programmes, share ideas for rewarding employees who attain green goals and support for being environmentally conscious. Employees must not be constrained to be part of the green team, but should try to find people who have instilled interest and enthusiasm for the issues. The green team should not just comprise the heads of departments, in fact, it tends to work way better as a multilevel taskforce, since more junior workers will see the wastage or flaws in the system that seniors might overlook. Moreover, top-level support and engagement is vital for a deeper commitment to sustainability to take hold.

Employees need to be encouraged to figure out how they can make a difference. The system should allow them to try out new ideas, organize zero-waste programmes, launch or sponsor local sports teams, raise money for disaster relief, serve meals to homeless or at-risk youth or participate in a fundraising walk. In addition, they can also be encouraged to suggest ways of saving energy or reducing waste in their day-to-day activities.

Communication and Inclusivity

There must be an annual plan with a designed event calendar that can be followed throughout the year. Employees may view environmental or social programmes as uninvited additions to an already-full workload. It is quite obvious that any employee would not like to add another chore to their list of work responsibilities, so it is vital to make the workplace enjoyable. Discussions on how the programmes relate to their roles is an important aspect here that needs attention.

Employees need to be educated on global warming, energy efficiency and recycling. There must be a session on invited speakers to share different aspects of the environment, including ways to incorporate environmentally sound actions into everyday living and thereafter.

There must be post signs that remind employees of the benefits of a green work environment. All the staff must be encouraged to give suggestions towards positive changes and must undergo to implement the best ones. This indicates to them that their ideas are being implemented, and management bothers to listen to them, consequently raises morale and increases environmental awareness.

Besides, dividing employees into teams, a competition can be organized in which employees and teams compete for prizes for their environmental stewardship or compete with other companies in a citywide competition. Each company can contribute a portion of its green savings to a charity or environmental non-profit group.

Leaders Are the Role Model

Managers must lead the way by demonstrating green behaviour. When employees see managers and owners practising conservation, they are more inclined to do themselves as well. When everyone in a company works together towards achieving green business objectives, theses practices become the norm instead of a burden.

The policies make corporate values explicit, clarifying expectations and help employees make better decisions. It is important to update your corporate values to include social and environmental goals and to publish 'green' goals on the website. In addition, the creation of policies and codes of conduct that support the goals and examples must be incorporated as 'green' successes in the company's annual report.

Moreover, the programme 'Green' must have the spirit of seeking the participation of all employees of varying seniority throughout the company. The programmes must be out from 'top-down' approach and should seek more buy-in from employees. Employees who are already passionate about environmental or social goals must be encouraged to build a 'green team'.

Creating a culture of creativity

- To create a culture that promotes a consistent time for creativity

- To stimulate more innovation, create a culture that nurtures creative flow and takes risks

- To explore nature to spark creativity

- To collect knowledge and experience from the available resources

- To dive in and move into the unknown territory

- To take risks without fearing of failures

- To ask for feedback

Last but not the least

For employers

- Cost reduction can be done through improved efficiency.

- Captivating and retaining the best and brightest talent is the key.

- The reputation and credibility among staff, consumers and investors improves the success of the programme systematically.

- There are multiple benefits of this initiative, some of which include enhanced market share and revenues from a stronger brand.

For employees

- There is a great opportunity to meet and work with people from other departments without the consideration of goal achievement and intra-professional rivalry and competition.

- There is a great opportunity to use practices learnt at work and at home, and subsequently to save money on personal bills as well.

- There is a great opportunity for learning as well as implementing new experiences outside the usual work and social environment.

- There is a chance of developing new skills and improved job satisfaction.

- There is an opportunity to involve in an issue that they are really concerned about.

Do you think TUSDAC is helpful?

Read more at https://members.tuac.org/en/public/topic/sd/index.phtml

Here, the example is shared of an employee who works in an organization that believes in encouraging green culture. The company has green HR policies and practices in the organization. The size of the organization is small, but the organization believes in the ethical way of working. The organization is pioneering in environment- and compliance-related facets. Here, the story of an employee is shared, how the organization's green practices influenced him becoming a 'green employee' by heart.

Mr Rajshekhar (name changed) started working at a manufacturing firm after completing his technical degree from a decent engineering college in India in mechanical stream. After completing his degree, he sat for interviews with three organizations. As Raj was a bright student and consistent throughout his academic career, he was selected in one organization through a campus selection process. He started working in the firm after completing his degree. As a positive and sincere student throughout his academic career, he also showed the same spirit and dedication towards his work, and soon became a favourite of many of his seniors. The company, though small, believes in the green way of working, particularly by complying with environment-related norms. The company used to give green KRAs to all engineers and managers, and a constant follow-up was also carried out. There was a suggestion scheme also. And all the suggestions given by the employees were assessed by a team of experts to evaluate their viability. One suggestion given by Raj was liked by the team of environmental experts and then implemented in the organization. This motivated Raj a lot, and he started taking even more interest in sustainability aspect. He began reading relevant literature and books on the topic. This influenced him a lot. Now, Raj is a completely transformed person. The impact is so much that it is reflected in his daily life. Some examples of his reformed behaviour are given further.

He carries a bag when he goes for shopping. When he buys new clothes, he tries to reuse the packing material like plastic cover in which the shirts, etc., were packed for keeping his important documents. This is the practice that helped saving the documents from termite and moisture in the rainy season. He started carrying his kits while purchasing some cooked food from a restaurant. His opinion is that the packing material used for packaging creates a lot of menace to the environment and is not good at all. He always carries a water bottle while travelling and refills it wherever he gets the opportunity for it. Thus, he does not need to buy packaged water bottle. This saves his money as well as reduces the usage of plastic overall. We all know that plastic is not good for health, and that food items or water stored in it for longer periods of time is harmful for health. The small steps taken by Raj are not only saving lots of resources but also are giving him some extra savings in his total monthly expenditure.

Lessons learnt

Evaluating the use of harmful plastic.

SUGGESTED READINGS

Aiman-Smith, L., Bauer, T., & Cable, D. (2001). Are you attracted? Do you intend to pursue, A recruiting policy capturing study. *Journal of Business and Psychology*, *16*(2), 219–237.

Bansal, P., & Roth, K. (2000). Why companies go green: A model of ecological responsiveness. *Academy of Management Journal, 43*(4), 717–736.

Barton, R. (2009). Is the grass any greener? *The Independent,* 8–13.

Boiral, O. (2002). Tacit knowledge and environmental management. *Long Range Planning, 35*(3), 291–317.

Brockett, J. (2006). Change agents. *People Management, 12*(23), 18–19.

Buysse, K., & Verbeke, A. (2003). Proactive environmental strategies: A stakeholder perspective. *Strategic Management Journal, 24*(5), 453–470.

Cadbury, A. (2006). Corporate social responsibility: Contemporary critiques. *21st Century Society, 1*(1), 5–21.

Carbon Trust. (2006). *Office based companies: Maximising energy savings in an office environment* (Report No. CT007). pp. 1–19. Carbon Trust.

Chartered Institute of Personnel and Development. (2009). B&Q reward cards to offer 3rd green benefit. *People Management,* 4.

Clarke, E. (2006). Power brokers. *People Management,* 40–42.

Cordia, J., & Sarkis, J. (2008). Does explicit contracting effectively link CEO compensation to environmental performance? *Business Strategy and the Environment, 17*(5), 304–317.

Cotton, C. (2008). *Go the green mile.* http://www2.people management.co.uk/pm/articles/gothegreenmile.htm?name=_guide&type=section

Davies, G., & Smith, H. (2007). Natural resources. *People Management,* 26–31.

Egri, C. P., & Herman, S. (2000). Leadership in the North American environmental sector: Values, leadership styles, and contexts of environmental leaders and their organizations. *Academy of Management Journal, 43*(4), 571–604.

Ehnert, I. (2009). *Sustainable human resource management.* Springer.

Felgate, G. (2006a). *U.K. employees set to drive greening of business.* Carbon Trust, 1–2.

Felgate, G. (2006b). Emission statements. *People Management,* 40–41.

Fernandez, E., Junquera, B., & Ordiz, M. (2003). Organizational culture and human resources in the environmental issue. *The International Journal of Human Resource Management, 14*(4), 634–656.

Fryxell, G. E., & Lo, C. W. H. (2003). The influence of environmental knowledge and values on managerial behaviours on behalf of the environment: An empirical examination of managers in China. *Journal of Business Ethics, 46*(1), 45–69.

Gardner, W. L., Aviolio, B. J., Luthans, F., May, D. R., & Walumbwa, F. O. (2005). Can you see the real me? A self-based model of authentic leadership and follower development. *Leadership Quarterly, 16*(3), 343–372.

George, B. (2003). *Authentic leadership.* Jossey-Bass.

Govindarajulu, N., & Daily, B. F. (2004). Motivating employees for environmental improvement. *Industrial Management and Data Systems, 104*(4), 364–372.

HEA. (2007). *Higher Education Academy, UK, Employable graduates for responsible employers (Cade, Student Force UK).* http://www.heacademy.ac.uk/ourwork/teachingandlearning/

alldisplay?type=projects&newid=esd/esd_employable_graduates
&site=york

Jabbour, C. J., Santos, F. C. A., & Nagano, M. S. (2010). Contributions of HRM throughout the stages of environmental management: Methodological triangulation applied to companies in Brazil. *The International Journal of Human Resource Management*, *21*(7), 1049–1089.

Jackson, S. E., & Seo, J. (2010). The greening of strategic HRM scholarship. *Organizational Management Journal*, *7*(4), 278–290.

Jackson, S. E., Renwick, D. W. S., Jabbour, C. J. C., & Muller-Carmen, M. (2011). State of the art and future directions for green human resource management: Introduction to the special issue. *German Journal of Research in Human Resource Management*, *25*(2), 99–116.

Madsden, H., & Ulhoi, J. P. (2001). Greening of human resources: Environmental awareness and training interests within the workforce. *Industrial Management and Data Systems*, *101*(2), 57–63.

May, D. R., & Flannery, B. L. (1995). Cutting waste with employee involvement teams. *Business Horizons*, *38*(5), 28–38.

Nidumolu, R., Prahalad, C. K., & Rangaswami, M. R. (2009). Why sustainability is now the key driver of innovation. *Harvard Business Review*, *87*(9), 57–64.

Parkes, C., & Borland, H. (2012). Strategic HRM: Transforming its responsibilities towards ecological sustainability: The greatest global challenge facing organizations. *Thunderbird International Business Review*, *54*(6), 811–824.

Phillips, L. (2007). Go green to gain the edge over rivals. *People Management*, *23*(9), 9.

Philpott, J., & Davies, G. (2007). *Labour market outlook* (Quarterly survey report, Summer). CIPD/KPMG, pp. 1–22.

Pirson, M., & Lawrence, P. (2010). Humanism in business: Towards a paradigm shift? *Journal of Business Ethics, 93*(4), 553–565.

Ramus, C. A. (2001). Organizational support for employees: Encouraging creative ideas for environmental sustainability. *California Management Review, 43*(3), 85–105.

Renwick, D. W. S., Redman, T., & Maguire, S. (2013). Green human resource management: A review and research agenda. https://work.chron.com/ways-encourage-employees-green-4470.html

Rothenberg, S., Pil., F. K., & Maxwell, J. (2001). Lean, green, and the quest for superior environmental performance. *Production and Operations Management, 10*(3), 228–243.

Roy, M. J., & Therin, F. (2008). Knowledge acquisition and environmental commitment in SMEs. *Corporate Social Responsibility and Environmental Management, 15*(5), 249–259.

Simms, J. (2007). Direct action. *People Management,* 36–39.

Stanwick, P. A., & Stanwick, S. D. (2001). CEO compensation: Does it pay to be green? *Business Strategy and the Environment, 10*(3), 176–182.

Stead, W. E., & Stead, J. G. (2004). *Sustainable strategic management.* M. E. Sharpe Inc.

TUC. (2009). *Go green at work: A handbook for union green representatives.* TUC.

TUSDAC. (2005). *Greening the workplace* (Discussion Paper). www.Defra.gov.uk/environment/tusdac/

Ulrich, D. (1997). *HR champions*. Harvard Business School Press.

https://nbs.net/p/engaging-employees-in-going-green-b12b68c1-bc1e-4e14-a9b9-a31e14297361

https://www.greenhotelier.org/our-themes/community-communication-engagement/engaging-employees/

https://e-csr.net/definitions/green-human-resources-management-meaning-definition/

https://www.greenimpact.com/best-practices-and-tools/employee-engagementsustainabilitymake-green-happen/

DISRUPTIVE AND SUSTAINABLE BUSINESS MODELS

The strategic business model (SBM) can be defined as 'a business model that creates competitive advantage through superior customer value and contributes to the sustainable development of the company and society' (Lüdeke-Freund, 2010, p. 23). Innovative business models for sustainability deliver positive results and significantly reduce negative impacts on the environment and society.

SBMs overpower the TBL perspective. SBM has its influence on a wide range of stakeholders' interests comprising the environment and society. The process helps in making changes in the organization's value-network creation in a manner that the deliverance of economic values is not much affected. They are crucial in operating and executing corporate innovations that can aid to engrain the sustainability for business processes along with gaining the competitive advantage.

Sustainable business models can be interpreted in many ways, for example, a business model that helps companies in terms of analysing, managing and communicating companies' sustainable worth manifesto to their stakeholders. These models are helpful for companies in creation and deliverance of values while maintaining or revitalizing natural, social and economic capital beyond their organizational boundaries (Schaltegger et al., 2016).

Business models help the company in transforming resources into economic value (Teece, 2010). It can be a sequence of components in value proposition such as product or service offering, customer segments, customer relationships, activities, resources, partners, distribution channels (i.e., value creation and delivery) or cost structure (Osterwalder & Pigneur, 2010).

As per Jackson (2009), organizations in sustainable economy are as follows:

- They are built on cooperation and sharing, rather than insisted competition.

- They promote restrictions on the consumption of natural resources, energy, water, goods, etc., by giving a feasible upper limit or by providing some substitutes.

- They try to magnify the societal and environmental benefits rather than systematizing economic growth.

- They have a closed-loop system where nothing is authorized to be wasted or discarded into the environment.

- They promote reuse, repairs and remakes.

- They emphasize the delivery of functionality and experience over the ownership of resources.

- They reward innovative practices and work experiences for all that augments human creativity and skills.

Business models guide the way that define its competitive strategy by designing the product or service on its market in an innovative way. Innovation out of it must also be economically feasible. These green innovative ideas help organizations in the long run. For example, the hybrid car model was introduced to capture attention in this direction, as it needs some regulatory changes as well.

GREEN INNOVATION

Green innovation is defined as 'innovations that consist of new or modified processes, practices, systems and products which benefit the environment and contribute to environmental sustainability' (Bocken & Allwood, 2012, p. 567).

> *For the future to be good, we need electric transport, solar power and (of course)...*
>
> **Elon Musk (@elonmusk) 29 April 2015 at Twitter[1]**

Tesla's CEO Elon Musk[2] did revolutionary work in this direction. He believed that fossil fuel substitutes need to be provided to society for reducing environmental harm. One of the products is batteries that can store electricity, which is pollution-free energy for homes, businesses and utilities.

As per Musk, while talking to Bloomberg, 'Our goal here is to fundamentally change the way the world uses energy, We're talking at the terawatt scale. The goal is complete transformation of the entire energy infrastructure of the world.'

Some other innovative models, such as Vertical Harvest as a concept, green and zero emission buildings, are discussed further.

---

[1] https://twitter.com/elonmusk/status/593296401196388352
[2] https://www.ecowatch.com/?s=elon+musk

VERTICAL HARVEST

'The Vertical Harvest farm' is an example of green innovation. It is a three-storey hydroponic greenhouse with an area measuring '30 feet by 150 feet plot' of land in Jackson, Wyoming. This green plot produces 37,000 pounds of greens, 4,400 pounds of herbs and 44,000 pounds of tomatoes. These innovative ways of farming 'sky-high farms' are good solutions to places where traditional farming is not possible. And local persons need not to depend always on pre-packaged foods that are high in fat and calories. The absence of fresh food replaced by pre-packaged food leads to obesity, diabetes and heart diseases. These forward-thinking ideas are the solution for attaining nutritious and healthy meals. Other than providing fresh and nutritious food, these vertical farms are capable of growing 'Caliber Biotherapeutics' in Bryan, a tobacco-like plant in vertical farms to make new drugs and vaccines.

It is seen that sustainable business models can serve as a vehicle to consolidate technological and social innovations. Sustainable manufacturing or, in general, sustainable business models safeguard the environment, along with continuously improving the condition of human life. The most vital challenge is sketching business models in such a way that enable the firm to capture economic value for itself while delivering social and environmental benefits (Schaltegger et al., 2012).

Green innovations such as eco-design and eco-efficiency improvements have aided in reduction of energy, resource intensity, and emissions and waste per unit of production. It is noted that, with these efforts, companies utilize less natural resources, which are almost 40 per cent less in five years in terms of energy utilization (Evans et al., 2009).

An Example of Smart/Green Building

As per Bloomberg, Deloitte's 'Amsterdam headquarter' is 'the smartest building in the world'.[3] This building uses around 28,000 sensors to monitor the efficient usage of light, temperature, moisture and movement. Even its employees use their smartphones to take coffee, etc. The LED panels used in this building produce more energy than they consume. It also saves energy in the unoccupied spaces in the building.

Zero-emission Building

Archiblox, an Australian architecture firm, has an intention to make carbon-positive homes. Residential and commercial buildings in Australia consume a larger percentage of total energy consumption. With this mission, the company came up with 'The Archiblox Carbon Positive House'. These houses are efficient and they can put energy back on the grid. Thus, Southern California's North Fontana area with such homes can create at least 20 such homes with a net zero energy consumption.

The London School of Economics (LSE), an academic institution, started a sustainability journey in a structured way since 2005. Management has come out with the environment policy. Initially, the institution had taken the target of reducing carbon emissions by 54 per cent by 2020. LSE installed PV and combined heated power (CHP) units in the buildings. Next step, as per Jon Emmett, Sustainability Projects Officer, was to 'ensure the redevelopment of the Centre Buildings and make it sustainable as much as possible to complete the efficiency target as committed'.[4]

---

[3] https://www.bloomberg.com/features/2015-the-edge-the-worlds-greenest-building/
[4] blogs.lse.ac.uk/sustainability@StudyLSE

SUSTAINABLE PRACTICES ACROSS THE BOARD

Leading organizations in the world such as the World Business Council for Sustainable Development (WBCSD), the United Nations Industrial Development Organization (UNIDO), the World Bank, the United Nations Environment Program (UNEP) and major international non-governmental organizations (INGOs) are working together in the field of SD to deliver some of the innovative sustainable models.

If we take the example from India, 'the Environment (Protection) Act' came into existence in 1986 with the objective of providing protection and improvement to the environment. It empowers the central government to establish authorities (under Section 3[3]) charged with the mandate of preventing environmental pollution in all its forms and to tackle specific environmental problems that are peculiar to different parts of the country. The Act was last amended in 1991. There are six reporting provisions in India that are solely concerned with waste, with special regulations existing for e-waste and plastic.

In addition, the top 500 listed companies on the National and Bombay Stock Exchanges in India are required to produce business responsibility reports (BRRs) which are to be included in their annual reports. Regulations require India's largest public companies to disclose a wide and diverse set of sustainability criteria—from GHG emissions and sexual harassment to stakeholder engagement. The decision by the Securities and Exchange Board of India (SEBI) in 2017 to ask top 500 listed companies to voluntarily adopt the integrated reporting framework is a positive recent development that should encourage the disclosure of non-financial information alongside financial information. Publishing such ESG information and data in the mainstream report brings it to the attention of investors and shareholders, and allows a wider, more sustainable conception of value to be fostered.

STATES GOING GREEN

Green initiatives with the National Mission for Green India under the Ministry of Environment, which approves four states, are an important thrust to the great cause. The perspective plan along with annual plans of operation and the National Executive Councils of Kerala, Mizoram, Manipur and Jharkhand are approved in this direction. Under this, NGOs and local organizations will work together and take an active stride since the inception, which includes the planning, decision-making, implementation and monitoring of the project. This is a perfect example of a diverse partnership among key stakeholders. This has multiple outcomes in the positive direction of job creation, along with 'enhancing the country's diminishing forest cover and responding to climate change by a combination of adaptation and mitigation measures'.

Some key facts about the Green India Mission are as follows:

- The 'Green India Mission' aims to increase forest cover to 5 million hectares.

- It also aims to preserve ecological services such as biodiversity, hydrological services, carbon appropriation and to regulate the collection of forest items such as fuel, fodder, timber and other forest produces.

- The initiative will also improve the livelihoods of around 3 million households around the country.

- The Green India Mission has been merged with the Union Ministry's Mahatma Gandhi National Rural Employment Guarantee Scheme, which has taken initiatives such as water harvesting, afforestation and farm forestry.

- Future plans are being made to execute pre-plantation, pit digging, planting and watering, fencing, plant support and protection activities, weeding, mulching and fertilization.

Source: India Today (2014).

DIVERSE PARTNERSHIP

Another initiative that needs a mention here is the 'LAUNCH' programme, in which companies such as Nike, NASA, USAID and the Department of State are part of it. LAUNCH tries to assess and solve global issues related to water, health, energy, waste and systems. This is indeed an example of a truly diverse partnership among representatives of business, government and scientific organizations. But one needs to understand that to solve a mega global-level issue, such a partnership is must and it states an example to others to come forward in the line of these innovations.

One more in the list includes the 'Sustainability Accounting Standards Board', which helps in connecting senior executives from big companies of the world for identifying specific environmental and social issues in different sectors. For example, challenges in the health sector related to supply chain may not be the same as other industries or sectors.

Along with this, there are companies that ingrain sustainability in their value system as a total integrated approach. They believe in having an attitude where all stakeholders are actively involved towards achieving the goals. This includes assigning of competitive and aggressive environmental goals to its employees. Each time they revisit, the existing bars are raised.

This ultimately results in healthy competition and better environmental performance.

An example of a company can be quoted here, that is, 'Patagonia', having a green mission. The company came into existence in 2011. It is an outdoor clothing retail company. Since its inception, the company is conscious towards the environment and sustainability, and it takes various steps to ensure that all processes at Patagonia's manufacturing are green. The company announced its 'Footprint Chronicles'. The company informs its consumers about every step of the processes of manufacturing digitally, thus allowing them to make informed decisions about the products they purchase.

Some of the other practices followed by *Patagonia* are discussed further.

The company believes in clear communication with employees and shares transparently the eco-friendly practices followed by the company. It does not hesitate to disclose the facts or hide facts where it is not able to maintain eco-friendly practices with its products, as some of the processes have to rely on fossil fuels.

Some of the other companies on the list are Coca-Cola, Lego, Dell and many others. For example, Dell's '2020 Legacy of Good Plan'[5] aimed to reduce its GHG emissions by 50 per cent and carbon value chain emissions by 25 per cent per drink; in addition to collecting back almost 75 per cent of bottles and cans, and replenishing almost 100 per cent of the water used by the company. Lego had taken a pledge to use 100 per cent renewable energy. Diageo could cut almost 80 per cent of its Greenhouse gases (GHG) emission in North America.

---

[5] http://i.dell.com/sites/doccontent/corporate/corp-comm/en/Documents/2020-plan.pdf

Examples of self-regulation and goals include, for example, the goal of Walmart to phase out its 10 of the most toxic chemicals it uses, the goal of HP to reduce carbon emission by 20 per cent in its supply chain, etc.

Some of the other companies in the list are Unilever, LinkedIn, Google, Apple, Unilever, P&G, Microsoft, Facebook, Amazon, PepsiCo, Shell, McKinsey, Nestlé, Johnson & Johnson, BP, GE, Nike, Pfizer, Disney, Coca-Cola, Chevron, L'Oréal, etc. In this list, some of the companies that are appreciated by their prospective and existing employees and customers are McKinsey and 'Shell'. If we talk of brand performance in the area of social and environmental goals, Unilever, though less valuable in terms of brand value, but is many a times ranked ahead of much better known brands than Disney, Nike and Coca-Cola.

The aforementioned examples reflect the continuous efforts of diverse stakeholders, such as the government, NGOs or private organizations, towards achieving environmental and sustainability in many ways. In order to address the issue, different models are adopted that not only help organizations reduce their carbon footprints but also help them in resource and cost saving. This needs a structured thinking throughout the process of the organization. Some of the business models as adopted by the organizations are discussed in detail in order to establish the link.

Do you know how Lean Quality Circles help in reducing waste in the supply and manufacturing chain?

Read more at https://qcfi.in/lean-quality-circle/

BUSINESS MODELS

Innovative business models that are followed across industries, are, for example, Lean Manufacturing (Melton, 2005), Natural Capitalism (Hawken et al., 2005), Social Enterprises (Grassl, 2012), Product Service Systems (Mont & Tukker, 2006; Tukker, 2004), New Economy Concepts (e.g., Blue Economy; Pauli, 2010), etc. Business model innovations for sustainability may not be economically viable initially, but later on the benefits can be reaped with this, 'the first hybrid car', which was noticed later when regulatory or other changes were seen.

In the following section, business models and examples of different companies involved in providing sustainable practices are discussed.

One of the models is 'Lean Manufacturing', which identifies and pertains to lessen waste in production processes (Melton, 2005; Shah & Ward, 2003). Waste, in this context, is not only seen as physical, material and energy waste but also takes care of excess production, material handling, excess processing, inventory defects and rework. The focus of Lean has attained substantial improvements in energy and material efficiencies and productivity improvements. For instance, 'Toyota production system' (Womack & Jones, 1996) summarizes the integration of Lean thinking throughout the business. Cleaner production concepts build on this and specifically focus on the reduction of waste and emissions from production processes.

Another model is Natural Capitalism (Hawken et al., 2005; Weizsäcker et al., 1997). It is a more specific approach towards sustainability. Under this, there is a need for radical transformation in energy efficiency and material productivity, rather than small incremental improvements.

It is found that with 'environmentally benign materials and production processes', chemical dyes are replaced with organic/benign dyes in textile production. Some of the other emerging changes include 'green chemistry' which aims to use naturally occurring processes in place of traditional industrial processes. For instance, it aims to imitate 'how spiders weave exceptionally strong webs using only organic materials and ambient pressure and temperatures, rather than the typical industrial processes that involve high energy inputs and environmentally damaging chemicals and acids'.

Substitute with renewables and natural processes archetype can be defined as reduced environmental impacts that enhance business elasticity by addressing resource constraints. The model limits the utilization of possessions related with non-renewable resources in the current production system. This archetype aims to reduce the environmental impacts of industry by substituting with renewable resources and natural processes to create significant environmentally benign industrial courses. It contributes to the wider need by limiting unwanted waste and pollution by replacing metals with natural and fibre-based materials through system-level renewable power generation systems.

The concept of 'waste' is eliminated by transforming waste streams into useful and valuable inputs to other production system, resulting in better use of underutilized capacity. Waste was selected as an archetype to seek improvements in efficiency and depleting waste and emissions. This model is different from the 'efficiency archetype', which operates on reducing waste to minimum. It seeks to recognize and create contemporary value from what is currently perceived as waste. This approach has similarities with the practical approach, where the concept of waste does not really exist, as all the 'waste' is transformed either into 'food stock' for any other resource that can further be utilized for some other process (Boons & Lambert, 2002; Gibbs & Deutz, 2007).

If we talk about some *country*-level innovative practices, 'Natural Solar Initiative' by Australia comes into this list. It commits to Australian citizens living with disabilities a 'Specialist Disability Insurance Scheme', in which affordable solar-powered housing for Australians are provided. Under this scheme, the cost of electricity goes down with the efficient use of electricity with battery and solar integration property. Persons with disabilities receive insurance under the National Disability Insurance Scheme.

Emission-free Transportation

This solar-powered electric bike is popular in America. As cities encourage people for using electric bikes, EcoWatch is an amazing substitute for this purpose. These bikes use solar cells on the wheels that send renewable energy directly to the bike's battery. On a full charge, it can go up to 30 mph. One of the popular bikes is the 'Solar Bike',[6] created by Danish solar engineer Jesper Frausig, which is powered by the clean, green energy of the sun.

Some other examples include cargo bikes, that is, Segway with pedals, 'Adam' concept bike with a detachable battery/speakers/navigation unit/power outlet on the handlebar that works—and looks like—a perfectly normal bicycle when the battery pack is taken off.

---

[6] http://solar-bike.weebly.com/the-solarbike.html

3D Printing

The Perpetual Plastic Project is a concept based on the making of products after recycling used plastics. Recycled plastic bottles, cups and other stuff that too often ends up in landfills[7] are shredded and turned into filaments fed into a 3D printer to produce objects like plastic rings. This technology has been touted as a solution to many of the planet's pressing problems, which is almost 13 per cent of US municipal solid waste stream.

Other innovators are using 3D printers to create nutritious food to help in reducing the global food waste crisis, and the company Pembient is using 3D printing to make fake rhino horns to stop poaching and save the rhino from going extinct!

Industrial symbiosis is a process adaptation solution that turns waste products from one process into feedstock for another process or product line (Ayres & Simonis, 1994; Chertow, 2000). The most famous example of industrial symbiosis is the industrial park Kalundborg (Chertow, 2000).

In the process, systems become more open and innovative. Structures are relooked, and new and improved production systems unfold a structure that incentivizes less resource utilization.

It also results in the promotion of upgraded cost-effective technologies and systems, thus resulting in an innovative business model with lots of opportunities (e.g., recent widespread uptake of solar photovoltaic panels). Local renewable energy solutions such as solar electricity provision in developing markets (e.g., for light, cookers) and using on-site windmills and solar power supply to initiate electricity for manufacturing processes

---

[7] https://www.ecowatch.com/beyond-reduce-reuse-recycle-to-a-world-without-waste-1881887019.html

(manufacturing examples are included in the work of Evans et al., [2009]) are some examples.

Another is the delivering of functionality, under this, rather than having ownership of all resources, services are hired that satisfy the needs of users without owning physical products. Under this, companies shift their business model from offering a manufactured product to offering a combination of products and services. This archetype is also about moving substantially towards a 'pure service model', that is, delivering functionality on a pay-per-user basis instead of disposing ownership of a product. While doing so, this may fundamentally evolve the material throughout the requirements of the industrial system.

Under this process, underutilized assets as a form of waste value are recaptured through shared ownership and collaborative consumption approaches. Examples of collaborative consumption approaches are used to radically reduce material throughout the process. Some of the emerging practices include 'peer-to-peer car sharing' and 'local community peer-to-peer electrical power tool sharing schemes'.

The potential benefits of this approach can be utilized with better coordination of customer and society needs with those of the manufacturer. It breaks the link between profit and production volume and diminishes the consumption of resources. It also deals with motivation and opportunity to collide with through-life and end-of-life issues as the manufacturer retains ownership of assets with increased efficiency. Some of the other added benefits are improved product longevity/durability and reuse of most of the materials in the process. This archetype has the potential to evolve consumption patterns, especially by reducing the need for product ownership. In fact, it encourages manufacturers to develop products that last longer and rebuild for upgradability and reparability, potentially reducing resource utilization.

The closed-loop business model (Winkler, 2011) comprises products and business processes sketched in such a manner that waste can be turned into a new transformed substance. An example of a closed-loop business model is 'interface floor providing office floor carpet tiles' (Anderson & White, 2011).

Cradle-to-Cradle (McDonough & Braungart, 2002) includes the idea of a closed-loop technical nutrient cycle with a biological open-loop cycle. The latter recognizes that it is not always possible to recollect material lost during the production and usage phase and, in such instances, these waste streams and emissions are designed to be environment friendly towards contributing positive nutrients to the natural environment.

The Ocean Cleanup

The company 'Ocean Cleanup' was started by Boyan Slat, a 20-year-old former aerospace engineering student. He felt deeply that plastic is a major threat to marine life and marine ecosystems. He estimated that the damage to the ecosystem was almost about $13 billion each year. Thus, he thought of doing a project to clean up the Great Pacific Garbage Patch with his Ocean Cleanup project. The project involved

> a static platform that passively corrals plastics as wind and ocean currents push debris through V-shaped booms. Floating filters then catch all the plastic off the top three meters of water where the concentration of plastic is the highest, while allowing fish and other marine life to pass under without getting caught. Some have described the project as the 'world's first feasible concept to clean the oceans of plastic.

Another example can be taken here of a sports company 'Adidas', which had developed shoes and clothes made from trash that was recovered from the ocean. The company also tried in a phased manner not to use plastic bags in its retail stores around the world.

Another example is the result-oriented price product service, where the system is based on payment per work. For example, Xerox Inc's provision of photocopying services (Baines et al., 2007) is based on customer payment per print, which discourages printing. In the similar lines, an example of car sharing (e.g., lease) while maintaining contracts and extended warranties (Tukker, 2004) can be quoted here.

The other form is adopting stewardship role, in which the archetype refers to actively engaging with all stakeholders to ensure their long-term health and well-being. Upstream stewardship examples comprise the Marine Stewardship Council (MSC, 2012), the Forestry Stewardship Council (FSC, 2012) and the Better Cotton Initiative. The traits of such business models are usually a supplier accreditation programme that denotes more ethical or sustainable business practices at grassroots level, usually in lower-middle income nations. The programmes deliver environmental and social sustainability initiatives such as employee welfare and living wages, community development (education, health, livelihoods), sustainable growing and harvesting of food and other crops, depleting chemical fertilizers and pesticides, water consumption and top soil erosion, environmental resources and biodiversity protection and regeneration.

In particular, the consumer pays a price premium to fund the benefit in the supply chain, motivated by the intangible value associated with such purchasing. Models generally appeal to consumer values, involving the consumer in supply chain issues instead of the retailer or manufacturer funding the premium (Fairtrade, 2011).

The downstream stewardship example comprises proactively tackling health issues of consumers. This is specifically relevant in the food, beverage and tobacco sectors, where health issues arise due to modern diets with over consumption combined with increasingly sedentary lifestyles. The sufficiency archetype aims to address this by resolving sustainability from the stance of sustainable consumption. For instance, energy-saving companies optimize the energy consumption of companies and public buildings. The savings achieved out of that are further used to reward the stakeholders involved (FORA, 2010).

Organizations also benefit for actively engaging in demand-side management, such as numerous-reputational benefits, risk reduction and avoiding scale-up costs. Government regulations play an important role in driving sustainable consumption (Schrader & Thøgersen, 2011). Frugal business models especially concentrate on the provision of products and services to low-income markets, often in extreme poverty. Business models take complex product concepts and rebuild them to reduce their base functionality. This involves eliminating superfluous or overly complex functionality and cosmetic features to provide products that use minimal materials and energy at minimal costs (Karamchandani et al., 2011).

Sustainable Practices (Examples from Indian Companies)

This section talks about some of the Indian organizations that are doing great as sustainable organizations towards making a change to the society.

The company 'Avani' is located in Kumaon region Uttarakhand. The company is committed to social development with local empowerment. The company had taken initiatives with community development programmes to create opportunities for rural women and men with very limiting sources of income, that is, agriculture for supporting large families. It supports them in finding options for employment through a self-sufficient and environmentally sustainable supply chain. It encourages conservation-based livelihood generation for rural communities.

The other company in this list is 'Replenish Earth', which runs a worldwide movement for supporting and facilitating sustainable, social businesses. The company follows the principles of the World Replenish Index, a marketplace that transcends and includes GDP to 100 per cent compostable products conscious of our environmental impact. The company invests towards a green, circular economy and believes in the philosophy of living in harmony with nature.

Another company in this list is 'Greenobazaar' from Gujarat. The company believes in giving a healthy life to everyone by providing organic, eco-friendly products at the convenience of the buyer by ensuring delivery at the doorstep.

'Daily Dump' founded in 2006 in Karnataka, is an innovative and design-thinking company, which works on a constantly re-imagining relationship with the earth, and with urban spaces. The motive is to adapt and change the 'mindsets about "waste," marginal livelihoods and about whose job it is to take care of "waste," how we can be harmless', etc. It helps in creating and imagining alternative scenarios that can help in changing the behaviour of users with the aim to reduce waste, improve material recovery and enable better livelihoods through voluntary collective action of urban citizens.

'Aspartika Biotech' a Bengaluru-based company, works on utilizing locally generated waste and by-products of agro-industries and palm oil industries and to develop value-added products like omega-3 fatty acids for human and animal application and feed additives for aqua, poultry cattle and pigs. The company received support from the Biotechnology Industry Research Assistance Council under the Biotechnology Industry Partnership Programme for scaling up the projects developed through big projects.

Oorja Energy Engineering[8] is a Hyderabad-based company specializing in providing sustainable solutions for industrial and commercial heating and cooling. The company provides products and solutions based on solar and energy efficiency. Fossil fuel consumption is greatly reduced or substituted by a product that is less harmful to the environment. The solutions are economically viable, moreover helps in reducing fossil fuel consumption.

Oizom from Gujarat, an environmental solution company, strives to create a sustainable living environment. The company does extensive R&D with the help of sophisticated data-driven solutions. The company specializes in making the prediction related to the consumption of natural resources such as air, water, soil and energy. The usage of technology makes predictions and measurements quiet accurate, thus helping to create a sustainable living environment.

'S4S Technologies' from Mumbai helps farmers by giving them advanced technology-driven food processing machines. These machines use S4S Technologies for preserving and making best quality processed food. The company uses Solar Conduction Dryer, Haldi Tech, SmartDry and Frost Dry technology.

GEM Enviro Management is another company that recycles waste to make t-shirts, caps and bags, and sells products

_____
[8] http://www.oorja.in/

under its brand 'Being Responsible'. The company was founded in 2013 by three motivated enthusiasts, Dinesh Parikh, Sachin Sharma and Aditya Parikh, who care for the environment and the waste pre- and post-consumer packaging material. These waste products are collected from factories, offices, hotels, motels and institutes in and around Delhi. Waste is then recycled into products for selling to consumers. Moreover, the company has also tried to run a number of awareness programmes to raise awareness about environmental sustainability and the importance of recycling in businesses, universities and institutes.

In 2017, two enthusiasts, Udit Sood and Nikita Barmecha, founded 'EcoRight', an initiative for providing trendy and eco-friendly products, such as designer bags, in Ahmedabad. The designs are trendy and they used e-commerce firm Amazon in India and the USA initially to promote their products. The company and its employees do not use any plastics in the office space and instead use biodegradable bags.

Another company that has taken small but important steps in this direction is TrulyMadly. This is an Indian dating and matchmaking app. The company was started in 2014 by Snehil Khanor and Sachin Bhatia. The start-up is extremely conscious towards the environment and sustainability. As per Snehil:

> Personally, I believe in reducing our carbon footprints whenever we can. We can do small things to achieve that. For example, I don't use my personal vehicle for daily work commute. I either travel via metro or carpool with friends and colleagues. Now, with electric vehicles coming up, I try and use it whenever I can.

Moreover, the company removed all plastic stirrers from the pantry and does not use plastic cups near the water cooler.

They do not use printer until it is very import, thus printing is restricted in the company, it is allowed only when it is absolutely necessary.

'We are also encouraging young employees to maintain plants. So, every quarter, along with a cash prize, we have started giving indoor plants to the winners. Little things like these bring bigger impact in the long term,' says Snehil.

NavAlt Solar & Electric Boats[9] is located in Kochi, India. The company tries to make marine transport more efficient by drastically reducing the energy and resources needed for building and operation. They have designed boats and ferries combining advancements in electrical vehicle technology, marine design and photovoltaics so that they run on solar energy.

NavAlt envisions a more efficient water transport system that does not use fossil fuels.

'Aadhan'[10] of Delhi NCR is a social enterprise trying to create an impact on recycled infrastructure space by recycling old shipping containers into eco-friendly, mobile infrastructure. They design buildings that can be sent to any location in the country. These structures are made from shipping containers retired from their tenure at sea and other environmentally friendly materials, emphasizing a culture of sustainability.

Gurugram-based 'The Man Company' is a male grooming start-up launched in 2015 by Bhisham Bhateja. According to the start-up, besides giving customers products that are beneficial to their aesthetic improvement, they are also meticulous about the ingredients they use. Their entire product range is free from harmful chemicals and is infused with essential oils.

---

[9] http://navaltboats.com/
[10] http://www.aadhan.org/

Bhisham says:

> We use 100 percent natural essential oils that are extrac-
> ted from herbs, flowers, seeds, and fruits. The manufac-
> turing of SLS has a drastic effect on the environment
> and using products containing SLS pollutes ground-
> water and results in bio-accumulation. All our products
> are free of this harmful chemical and parabens. We are
> also strictly against animal testing and our containers are
> recyclable.

The start-up also refrains from using plastics as much as possible in their office space, and all its packaging products are
recyclable. Speaking about being eco-friendly and how other
start-ups can do the same, Bhisham says:

> Eco-friendly for us means reducing the impact we have
> on the environment as much as possible. While we do
> have certain practices in place, the key one being not
> using any SLS or parabens. Although, they we know
> there is still a long way to go in this regard.

Desalination

An initiative by the Massachusetts Institute of Technology
and the Jain Irrigation Systems was taken to convert salt water
(brackish water) into clean drinking water using solar energy.
This *solar-powered*[11] machine is able to pull salt out of water and
further disinfect the water with ultraviolet rays, making it suit-
able for irrigation and drinking. This technology recently won
the top $140,000 Desal Prize from the US Department of the
Interior, which recognizes innovators who create cost-effective,

---

[11] https://www.ecowatch.com/?s=solar

energy-efficient and environmentally sustainable desalination technologies that can provide potable water for humans and water for crops in lower-middle income countries.

Increasing Global Awareness

The previous discussion showed that it seems that there is an increasing awareness globally. There are a number of initiatives taken at country level, organizational level as well as individual level. Many countries have come up with stricter norms in terms of resource utilization and recycling waste. Different organizations are devoted towards this concern. At the individual level also, we can find solutions as suggested. Thus, it is an urgent need to understand the importance of sustainability at each and every level. A bunch of organizations and persons cannot make the movement a success. Rather, when all stakeholders join hands together with providing and using innovative ways of handling the challenges, we may find enough reasons to make the planet liveable for our future generations.

REFERENCES

Anderson, R., & White, R., 2011. *Business lessons from a radical industrialist*. St. Martin's Griffin Press.

Ayres, R., & Simonis, U. (Eds.). 1994. *Industrial metabolism: Restructuring for sustainable development*. United Nations University Press.

Baines,T., Lightfoot, H., Evans, S., Neely, A., Greenough, R., Peppard,J., Roy, R., Shehab, E., Braganza, A., Tiwar, A., Alcock, J. R., Angus,J. P., Bast, M., Cousens,A., Irving, P Johnson, M., Kingston, J., Lockett, H., Martinez, V., Michele, P., Tranfield, D., Walton, J. P., & Wilson, H. (2007). State-of-the-art in product-service systems. Proceedings of the Institution of Mechanical Engineers Part B: Journal of Engineering Manufacture, *221*(10), 1543–1552.

Bocken, N., & Allwood, J. (2012). Strategies to reduce the carbon footprint of consumer goods by influencing stakeholders. *Journal of Cleaner Production, 35*, 118–129.

Boons, F., & Lambert, A. (2002). Eco-industrial parks: Stimulating sustainable development in mixed industrial parks. *Technovation, 22*(8), 471–484.

Chertow, M. R. (2000). Industrial symbiosis: Literature and taxonomy. *Annual Review of Energy and the Environment, 25*(1), 313–337.

Evans, S., Bergendahl, M., Gregory, M., & Ryan, C. (2009). Towards a sustainable industrial system. With recommendations from Education, Research, Industry and Policy. http://www. ifm.eng.cam.ac.uk/uploads/Resources/Reports/industrial_ sustainability_report.pdf

Fairtrade. (2011). *The Fairtrade foundation.* http://www.fair trade.org.uk/

FORA. (2010). Green business models in the Nordic region: A key to promote sustainable growth. http://www.foranet.dk/ media/27577/greenpaper_fora_211010.pdf

FSC. (2012). Forest Stewardship Council. http://www.fsc.org/

Gibbs, D., & Deutz, P. (2007). Reflections on implementing industrial ecology through eco-industrial park development. *Journal of Cleaner Production, 15*(17), 1683–1695.

Grassl, W. (2012). Business models of social enterprise: A design approach. *ACRN Journal of Entrepreneurship Perspectives, 1*(1), 37–60.

Hawken, P., Lovins, A. B., & Lovins, L. H. (2005). Natural capitalism: The next industrial revolution. Earthscan Ltd.

India Today. (2014). Four states to go green in India: All you need to know about Green India Mission. https://www.indiatoday.in/education-today/gk-current-affairs/story/green-initiative-268079-2015-10-14

Jackson, T. (2009). *Prosperity without growth: Economics for a finite planet.* Earthscan.

Karamchandani, A., Kubzansky, M., & Lalwani, N. (2011). Is the bottom of the pyramid really for you? *Harvard Business Review, 89*(3), 107–111.

Lüdeke-Freund, F. (2010). Towards a conceptual framework of business models for sustainability. In R. Wever, J. Quist, A. Tukker, J. Woudstra, F. Boons and N. Beute (Eds.), *Knowledge collaboration & learning for sustainable innovation.* Delft.

McDonough, W., & Braungart, M. (2002). Cradle to cradle: Remaking the way we make things. North Point Press.

Melton, T. (2005). The benefits of Lean Manufacturing what Lean thinking has to offer the process industries. *Chemical Engineering Research and Design, 83*(A6), 662–673.

Mont, O., & Tukker, A. (2006). Product-service systems: Reviewing achievements and refining the research agenda. *Journal of Cleaner Production, 14*(17), 1451–1454.

MSC. (2012). Marine Stewardship Council. http://www.msc.org/

Osterwalder, A., & Pigneur, Y. (2010). *Business model generation: A handbook for visionaries, game changers, and challengers.* John Wiley & Sons.

Pauli, G. (2010). *The blue economy. 10 years, 100 innovations, 100 million jobs* (Report to the Club of Rome). Paradigm Publications.

Schaltegger, S., Hansen, E. G., & Lüdeke-Freund, F. (2016). Business models for sustainability: Origins, current research, and future avenues. *Organization & Environment, 29*(1), 3–10.

Schaltegger, S., Lüdeke-Freund, F., Hansen, E. (2012). Business cases for sustainability: The role of business model innovation for corporate sustainability. *International Journal of Innovation and Sustainable Development, 6*(2), 95–119.

Schrader, U., & Thøgersen, J. (2011). Putting sustainable consumption into practice. *Journal of Consumer Policy, 34*(1), 3–8.

Shah, R., & Ward, P. (2003). Lean Manufacturing: Context, practice bundles, and performance. *Journal of Operations Management, 21*(2), 129–149.

Teece, D. (2010). Business models, business strategy and innovation. *Long Range Planning, 43*(2–3), 172–194.

Tukker, A. (2004). Eight types of product service system: Eight ways to sustainability? Experiences from SusProNet. *Business Strategy and the Environment, 13*(4), 246–260.

Weizsäcker, E., von Lovins, A., & Lovins, L. (1997). *Factor four: Doubling wealth halving resource use* (The New Report to the Club of Rome). Earthscan Publications Ltd.

Wells, P., & Seitz, M. (2005). Business models and closed-loop supply chains: A typology. Supply Chain Management: International Journal, *10*(3–4), 249–251.

Womack, J. P., & Jones, D. T. (2003). *Lean thinking: Banish waste and create wealth for your corporation* (2nd ed). Simon & Schuster.

Winkler, H. (2011). Closed-loop production systems: A sustainable supply chain approach. *CIRP Journal of Manufacturing Science and Technology, 4*(3), 243–246.

SUGGESTED READINGS

Brabham, D. (2008). Crowdsourcing as a model for problem solving: An introduction and cases. *Convergence, 14*(1), 75–90.

Chesbrough, H., & Crowther, A. K. (2006). Beyond high tech: Early adopters of open innovation in other industries. *R&D Management, 36*(3), 229–236.

Costanza, R., D'Arge, R., De Groot, R., Farber, S., Grasso, M., Hannon, B., Limburg, K., Naeem, S., O'Neill, R. V., Paruelo, J., Raskin, R. G., Sutton, P., & van den Belt, M. (1997). The value of the world's ecosystem services and natural capital. *Nature, 387*(6630), 253–260.

Dant, R. P., Grünhagen, M., & Windsperger, J. (2011). Franchising research frontiers for the twenty first century. *Journal of Retailing, 87*(3), 253–268.

Garetti, M., & Taisch, M. (2012). Sustainable manufacturing: Trends and research challenges. *Production Planning & Control, 23*(2–3), 83–104.

Lowitt, E. (2013). *The collaborative economy.* Jossey-Bass (Wiley).

Nerkar, A., & Shane, S. (2003). When do start-ups that exploit patented academic knowledge survive? *International Journal of Industrial Organization, 21*(9), 1391–1410.

Oltra, V., & Saint Jean, M. (2009). Sectoral systems of environmental innovation: An application to the French automotive industry. *Technological Forecasting Social Change, 76*(4), 567–583.

Osterwalder, A., & Pigneur, Y. (2005). Clarifying business models: Origins, present, and future of the concept. *Communications of the Association for Information Systems*, *15*(1), 1–25.

Randers, J. (2012). 2052: *A global forecast for the next forty years*. Chelsea Green Publishing, 376.

Richardson, J. (2008). The business model: An integrative framework for strategy execution. *Strategic Change*, *17*(5–6), 133–144.

Senge, P., Smith, R., Kruschwitz, N., Laur, J., & Schley, S. (2008). *The necessary revolution. How individuals and organizations are working together to create a sustainable world*. Nicholas Brealey Publishing.

https://www.business.com/articles/rise-of-green-business-innovation/

https://hbr.org/2013/12/2013-in-sustainability-the-year-business-got-off-the-sidelines

https://www.ecowatch.com/7-green-innovations-that-are-changing-the-way-we-do-business-1882037193.html

https://yourstory.com/socialstory/2019/10/eco-friendly-startups-workplace-green

https://saathipads.com/blogs/saathi/10-influential-and-sustainable-organisations-in-india...pic.twitter.com/8mwVW ukQDL

A GREEN WORKPLACE

> *You have to hold yourself accountable for your actions, and that's how we're going to protect the Earth*
>
> **Julia Butterfly Hill**

Environmentally sensitive, resource-efficient, socially responsible and strategically sustainable: Is this what a 'green workplace' looks like?

Just like Julia Butterfly Hill said, in today's times with the growing environmental consciousness, business houses either voluntarily or to meet stakeholders' expectations have adopted green practices. With SBMs in place and visionary leadership, it is not difficult to achieve. But the mammoth task is to make it happen. Every look and feel of the company must reflect the vision it shows, the mission it desires to achieve and the values it follows, be it the architecture and design of the building, the interior and the use of fittings or technology it devours, the employees it appoints, policies it brands or practices it shadows.

In earlier examples, we have observed that the geographical clustering of industries leads to several environmental consequences, such as air pollution and the depletion of oil supplies, water pollution and irrevocable loss of natural resources. The greening of organizations is full of opportunities, but it seems that there are some challenges too.

Smart organizations know how to ensure their core values. This can happen either by persuading their employees or by giving them a clear message that, for example, environmental and sustainability practices are as important as work performance. In today's knowledge economy, a lot of onus is on employees for taking the responsibility of growing, acclimatizing, refining and innovating the company. It is important that the message of a green work culture must be communicated from day one to all those who have to be held accountable for their actions.

Thus, the design of the workplace is such that it supports the basic and core idea in a more accommodating and comprehensive manner. When employees find the conviction among their leaders, they tend to behave in the manner that supports a green and sustainable way of working in an interrelated and interlinked way.

A GREEN WORKPLACE

A green workplace is an eco-friendly and focused organization and leans towards the adoption of business practices that are justifiable in nature, energy efficient and well suited to the complex as well as the ever-changing world of business.

It is not only green building and green infrastructure, rather it has a much broader scope. It encompasses green competencies, green attitude and green behaviour, which are combined synergistically to help the organization become green or sustainable.

In the series of examples under the green workplace, ITC hotels has set some of the best illustrations. Their green policies have been an important aspect in their practices for close to a decade now. In all their properties across the country, the commitment to *go green* has not only been substantiated by results but also has been recognized by those who are concerned.

ITC Hotels is the only company in the world of its size to achieve the environmental distinction of being water, carbon and solid waste recycling positive. Besides, it has become renowned example for delivering a luxurious yet sustainable experience for its guests at its properties throughout India. The group's commitment to 'responsible luxury' sets a benchmark for the industry as the first premium chain to achieve the prestigious LEED® Platinum rating for all its luxury hotels.

GREEN WORKPLACE IN ACTION

There are some key elements that need to be considered when we talk about a green workplace. It starts with developing infrastructure in such a manner that it utilizes natural resources without harming the overall environment. These are conscious efforts that even benefit the organization when it is intentionally integrated into its business operations, such as green design and layout, green construction and green operational practices of a company.

1. *Green design and layout:* Green or sustainable design and layout seeks to reduce negative impacts on the environment and health, and to ensure the comfort of occupants by improving building performance and reducing the consumption of non-renewable resources, minimizing waste and creating a healthy and productive environment.

2. *Green construction:* Green construction refers to creating structures using processes that are environmentally

responsible and resource efficient throughout a building's life cycle, starting from design, construction, operation, maintenance, renovation and deconstruction. It is designed to reduce the overall impact of the built-up environment on human health by efficiently using energy, water and other resources. It helps in protecting occupants' health along with improving employee productivity. Other aspects are related to reduction of waste, pollution and environmental degradation.

3. *Green operational practices:* Green operational practices refer to ensuring total energy efficiency and cutting down on wasteful resource use. Being a part of an organization, each employee must be given the responsibility for 'doing a bit' for the environment. Even small steps, such as installing energy-efficient light bulbs, can help in reducing carbon footprints, and subsequently *utility bills*. Some green operational practices may be adopted in an organization such as 'conserve water, recycle paper, turn off lights and electronics, when not in use', 'invest in a digital filing system, go energy efficient, install low-flow aerators that reduce water wastage, empower employees to sustainability, create a green team'.

> We can't just consume our way to a more sustainable world.
>
> **Jennifer Nini**

To understand better, few practices that showcase green workplace, starting with building certification, make the whole conversation more meaningful and relatable.

The certification for building, LEED, which is given when an infrastructure or a building has a design that focuses on and reduces the consumption of energy and other resources. Few examples of the companies are illustrated further.

CALCUTTA ELECTRIC SUPPLY CORPORATION, ENERGY COMPANY: PAVING THE WAY!

With respect to green workplace and infrastructure, Calcutta Electric Supply Corporation (CESC) is a perfect example. It has formed a *Going Green* committee and initiated the task of converting the CESC House into a green building in 2011 and later for facility improvement measures in various phases. Diverse trials have been taken to move the building towards the world-class green practices.

Further, a *green* workplace is one that significantly reduces or entirely nullifies the harmful effects on employees as well as the natural environment. It is made possible by incorporating eco-friendly operational strategies, adopting energy-saving technologies and paying attention to staff needs, sanitizing them and making them aware towards environmental harms.

Organizations need to focus upon some basic principles: (a) environmental protection, (b) economic development, (c) social development and (d) employee sensitization.

Do you know which are the most polluting industries in the world?

Read more at https://www.worldatlas.com/articles/the-top-10-polluting-industries-in-the-world.html

ENVIRONMENTAL PROTECTION

Buy less, choose well, make it last.

Vivienne Westwood

Environmental protection refers to any activity that seeks to protect, analyse and monitor the environment against the misuse or degradation from humans in order to maintain and restore the quality of the natural environment. Environmental protection is one of the basic principles of a sustainable or 'green' workplace.

1. Reducing and reusing the usage of products, thus saving the overall natural flora and fauna

2. Conserving and using sustainably the oceans, seas and marine resources

3. Recycling the residuals and making them usable for some other purpose

4. Ensuring sustainable consumption and production patterns

5. Prevention of the degradation of landscape and ecosystem, thus managing forests, combating desertification, halting and reversing land degradation and halting biodiversity loss

The journey of CESC is unique and a classic example of getting LEED certification. The corporate office of the company runs in the heritage building, which is 80 years old, and thus transforming the *corporate office* to *green office* was a real challenge for the stakeholders. One cannot make structural changes in the heritage building. Moreover, keeping its aesthetics and legacy intact while introducing towards green was a real challenge.

It was found that major renovations of the façade were not possible. Moreover, changes for the eco-friendly orientation had to be done wholly through non-structural renovations. Another point was that shifting and arranging of old drawing and data was a tedious and time-consuming exercise that also needed a lot of cost expenditure. Upgradation of an existing building as per green standards takes longer time compared to new construction. CESC had taken the firm decision on stepping up the resource constraints even though space was limited to accommodate today's sophisticated technological systems needed to obtain energy-savings criteria under the LEED rating system. In order to get the support of employees, a huge amount of time was spent on making them understand its importance. All these challenges and tireless efforts did not go in vein as these initiatives were recognized nationally in June 2014.

Another example in the series is the initiative of the CESC towards using solar reflective (SRI) paint on the roof. The SRI Paint is an excellent roofing material that reflects the sunlight and prevents the roof from getting heated. It can achieve attractive power saving of up to 40 per cent during peak summers in the areas where humidity is very high such as Kolkata.

SMALL EFFORTS CAN EVEN MAKE A BIG DIFFERENCE

The CESC also converted earlier used wooden windows to new sound- and heat-proof glass windows for utilizing better natural daylight. Also, trees were planted outside those windows to create green ambience in the building.

The CESC initiated low-flow water faucets in all toilets, initiating indirect energy savings via reducing the amount of water to be pumped. The installation of the water management system for the cooling tower turned into a major electricity saving with annual electricity savings.

Waste Management

Towards waste management efforts, the hotel has a system of separating different kinds of waste that are separated and disposed of suitably. For this purpose, they take the support of external bodies working in the field of environment and sustainability work with specialized services on waste segregation and management in a proper manner.

Anubhav Enterprises Goes Paperless

Anubhav Enterprises, a small trading enterprise, was founded by Anubhav Singh five years ago and has been doing well since its inception. Anubhav was very satisfied with the progress of the organization, but seemed very unhappy with how the office space looked. The office was of modest dimensions and was full of several reams of paper and files, and it seemed that the collection of paper would become unmanageable if not checked. He called a meeting of all employees with the agenda of converting the office into a paperless office without compromising on efficiency and loss of important information. He made a number of suggestions to his employees— they could stop receiving all forms of bills and invoices in paper form and send e-bills to their customers. Utility bills and bank statements could be received in digital form. He requested the IT officer to begin the process of digitizing all documents and old files. Anubhav stressed the importance of using technology such as Cloud and sharing of digital files and making them digitally accessible to employees. He announced his plan of not to replace malfunctioning printers and to reduce the number of printers to two that would be used in situations where printing on paper was unavoidable. He also announced a suggestion scheme for employees to share their ideas on how to make this new digital office workable. He further instructed the IT officer to ensure data security. He also shared the projected savings in paper over the next one year, which could be considerable.[1]

PLEDGE FROM WITHIN

There are some out-of-box ideas that are promoted by different institutions to promote a green initiative. Here, the example of a school is appropriate to mention.

This is the story of a school that recently appointed a new principal. She was very enthusiastic towards the environment and resource conservation. After joining the school, she made some arrangements that are worth applauding, and one can learn from them. Before making those ideas into practice, she initially discussed the notion among faculty and staff members. She explained how they were harming the environment and exploiting natural resources. She gave a task to all with a message 'can you suggest how in our campus we can improve sustainable practices'. Resources included paper, water, electricity, food and similar items. It was also proposed that they can make teams and can brainstorm the idea among themselves. They can start looking around and can realize how, without compromising the quality of day-to-day functioning, the use of resources can be minimized. Few days before the day of the next meeting, all teams were requested to send their proposals to the principal in a format as recommended by her. The principal received many proposals from both faculty and staff members. She studied all of them and selected

---

[1] https://www.profitbooks.net/how-to-create-paperless-office-10-tips-app-suggestions/

five best proposals. She requested all five teams to present their ideas in a general meeting where all the employees were present. This was a huge boost for all teams. All teams presented their proposals with lots of passion. The principal applauded all teams and publicized that she was touched by the eagerness and effort of all of them and thanked them for the gesture. She further announced that the ideas will be implemented in a phased manner in the institute. Apart from that, she also picked some of the ideas from the remaining proposed projects and applauded the members and the idea that she can apply in the institute in due course of time. The small exercise initiated by the principal resulted in saving a lot of paper, food, water, energy and so on. These were only small interventions or substitutes of existing processes. The employees themselves were exercising the responsibility of implementing the same in the organization. This was really a win-win situation for all without harming anyone. The staff and faculty felt that they are valued and felt pleased and proud that they are doing their bit for the environment.

THE JOURNEY JUST BEGUN

The aforementioned story was not the end here, rather it was a new beginning to achieve a green mission.

The whole exercise had multiple benefits.

The school started sending online weekly newsletters to the parents, which were sent offline earlier (and classroom news-letters). There was an immediate impact and paper usage was reduced to zero. Earlier, the practice was to send a note to parents, and the student had to get it signed to ensure that they received the information. Thus, the school had sent e-mails and WhatsApp messages and normal messages to all parents and did the survey as which mode of communication they found more convenient for them. Moreover, it was discussed with parents in the parent–teacher meeting (PTM). Once it was ensured by the parents that online medium is convenient for them, it became a practice in the school to communicate with the parents through messages or e-mails. After receiving the communication from schools, parents needed to reply them back so that teachers and staff of the school could be ensured that the message was received and acknowledged by the parents. After that, this became the regular practice for sharing all important information related to field trips, fan-outs, PTM updates, volunteer requests, etc.

The next step taken by the school was to organize a large fair in the school and to announce many competitive events with attractive prizes. These events were related to making usable products from the waste material. This was taken with great fervour by participating kids from different schools. And students created products, such as musical rumba shakers from drinkable yogurt containers, containers for keeping different stationery and folders for keeping papers using strips of outdated newspaper, yogurt containers, old piggy banks, matchboxes, ice-cream strips, etc.

Moreover, an idea was floated in the school itself and a library for old books and magazine was created, where students could donate their used books, magazines, extra stationery, CDs, pen drives, etc. These items could be borrowed or used by anyone at any point of time. Students were given responsibility for managing the library. They were also encouraged to participate in local, state, national and international events where they could showcase their talent for making usable products or reusing existing products with additional benefits.

This complete exercise was taken with great passion by all the stakeholders associated with the school. This gave multiple paybacks to the institute. The brand of the school was amplified, the faculty, staff and students acclaimed lots of love and respect from society. The school could win various awards and certificates further.

Thus, why not, we all can make small steps in this direction and can make the world a better place to live in.

LEMON TREE STANDS TALL AND GREEN

Aerocity building of Lemon Tree is LEED certified. The infrastructure layout is designed in such a manner that it improves efficiency with well-*insulated* and more *airtight* construction to limit heat losses in the winter along and light with proper ventilation. First in the list is focus on increased ventilation. This results in increasing the airflow with less airborne infections. When the natural airflow is more, it automatically prevents the generation of bacteria, moulds or other fungi.

Another aspect is building an enveloping design capable of managing moisture sources from outside and inside. For controlling indoor humidity, effective heating, ventilating, air-conditioning (HVAC) is in place. These are the systems that are followed in most of the studied organizations for this book and detailed discussions are mentioned in the other subsections. The entire building of Lemon Tree Aerocity has a centralized HVAC system, but with multiple controls, which enables it to switch off or adjust the power in places wherever needed.

They believe in the TBL concept by complying with all statutory requirements. In all Lemon Tree hotels, they have a sewage treatment plant (STP) and an RWH plant available.

'We want to build an organization of highly engaged, productive and diverse professionals who find opportunities to give back to society. We recruit hearing and speech impaired people who will make 10 per cent of the workforce by end 2013,' as mentioned by Mr Keswani. He further added that at Lemon Tree, they reuse, recycle and replenish the resources used by building hotels to LEED's silver and gold standards through environment-friendly practices in general. By doing this, Lemon Tree will be one of India's most cost-effective hotel companies. He further said, 'Lemon Tree wants to retain the competitive advantage of best-in-class business model with lowest costs, superlative service delivery and revenue maximization.'

Lemon Tree not only adheres to the mandatory requirement from statutory bodies but also keeps on learning and innovating in terms of adopting sustainable and green practices in all their hotels. At Lemon Tree hotels, many steps have been taken to bring down power consumption or use renewable energy (wind power is being implemented in a phased manner at Chennai property, followed by Aurangabad and Pune). 'Reducing power consumption is a key priority. Our hotels are designed so that entire floors can be shut down if demand drops (unlike others, our AC and water lines are horizontal)', said Mr Keshwani.

'Apart from the usual, we also use water from STP for cooling towers. Sensors and flow restrictors notwithstanding, area-wise metering of water consumption is undertaken to determine areas of high usage and initiate further conservation methods.' Patu Keswani, CMD, Lemon Tree Hotels, shares that they use approximately 30 per cent of the recycled water from STP in garden and flush systems. We also use other techniques and alternate sources to save energy. For example, 'Key Tag Energy Saver System, Solar Panel for hot water, Wind Power and many more,' as per Mr Keswani.

Next comes reducing the usage of energy by giving the design in such a manner that follows the sun. This helps in improving interior illumination through getting more daylight.

Also, the technology and systems used must be energy efficient for reducing computer glare.

Taj Hotels Monitors Indoor Environment's Health

Another company under the hospitality industry has come up with lots of new practices. Here, we are talking about the *TAJ Delhi* hotel. Taj had put systems in place (health checkers) that continuously monitor the health of the indoor environment. These systems, for example, are available in Taj New Delhi to monitor and display the level of carbon dioxide inside the hotel. Other systems monitor the availability of daylight, reduction of glare, thermal/individual comfort, etc.

ITC's Majestic Wind Farms

Again, the example from ITC Hotels about their practices of having wind farms is worth mentioning here. These wind farms produce as much energy as enough to light up the Delhi–Mumbai Highway for one year. Hot water generated at ITC Hotels through the use of solar energy would be sufficient to address the average hot water consumption of 6,000 households/families.

ITC Gardenia uses frontier green technologies in its systems such as water recycling, energy and waste management, along with eco-friendly materials in its architecture and décor. The wood used in the hotel has been outsourced from the Forest Stewardship Council, which is certified not to be from natural forests, but from special forests grown for this purpose. Also, 74 per cent of the wood, including the flooring, is made out of engineered wood using wood dust. These have been made into cedar-finished ply.

Extensive use of CO_2 sensors is in place for improving indoor air quality and ventilation. In the STPs, there are separate treatments for black and grey water and with ultraviolet equipments, there is a reduction in maintenance cost. Not only that, their commitment to greener practices also extends to the services they offer, that is, from green banquets to green conferencing.

The Oberoi and Their Water Conservation Revolution

The initiatives taken by *the Oberoi*, Mumbai, also serve as an easy example.

The Oberoi, Mumbai, is an excellent example of how they manage their water resource efficiently.

As per Mr Bharma, Executive VP, the Oberoi audits energy consumption on a day-to-day basis.

> Sub-meters monitor targets, and control power consumption for strategic areas. Energy benchmarks for daily operation volumes of various departments have been set, and performance is monitored on the daily basis. The benchmarks are reviewed quarterly for further scope of improvement. Energy audits had been conducted and methods of improvement in energy efficiency are being implemented.

For controlling energy consumption and enhancing energy efficiency, *variable refrigerant volume* technology for air conditioning is used as an integrated room automation system. In addition, heat recovery ventilation with thermal enthalpy wheels, light-emitting diode (LED) lighting in public areas, etc., are also added in this direction. Mr Bharma explains:

> We have the world's most energy efficient and lowest emissions Trane CenTraVac chillers in air-conditioning systems. Their energy consumption is as low as 0.57 KW per ton. The hotel also uses halon-free fire extinguishers and chimney stack heights are maintained according to Pollution Control norms.

Printed stationery of the hotel, which is one side blank, is otherwise reused as notepads or for photocopying, facsimile printouts and posters for internal use.

The vegetation waste is segregated from other non-degradable waste and further shredded and used for making compost. Non-degradable waste, such as polythene bags, is used for plant propagation purposes and is reused after plants are transplanted.

The engine oil that lubricates the wheels of hand carts, trolleys and banquet set-up garbage is handed over to the agency that builds huts and sheds for poor people.

Marriott: Responsible Hospitality with Improved Guest Experience

Marriott International, another example from the hospitality industry, has demonstrated the way to 'responsible hospitality'. The example can be quoted when we talk about economic development, but not at the cost of the environment and sustainability. The example can be seen as a positive force towards the desired direction in terms of formulating environment-friendly policies and practices.

The strategy of the hotel is to reduce the environmental impact by adding innovative ideas and advanced technologies. In total, it is seen that guest experience is even enhanced while hotels are projected to be environmentally sustainable hotels.

It needs an integrated approach from top to bottom and must be ingrained in the core values and culture of the organization. For example, the hotel has incorporated and integrated building automation systems and other automated controls to increase the efficiency of buildings. It also *installs smart, integrated occupancy thermostat systems that interlock with entry doors and property management systems to deliver agile temperature setback efficiency without impacting guest comfort and preference.*

Marriott follows 'chilled water diagnostic tool' in many properties in America. This is an opportunity for identifying water savings and cost consumption in the production of chilled water. The 'Demand Response Program' is the process where the total saving of resources is incentivized to encourage the practices of managing and efficiently utilizing grid-supplied electricity during times of peak demand.

Lighting retrofits provide energy efficiency opportunities as newer technology lowers replacement costs, and systems are upgraded in all properties around the world. Moreover, for assessing and audit purpose, Marriott hires consultants for third-party studies on retro-commissioning efforts for more complex facilities. These auditing and third-party bodies are incorporated to manage efficiency for HVAC, chiller and boiler systems. In addition, if they may get some option where renewable energy can be used or an opportunity for on-site energy generation with the help of windmill, etc., those are considered as best practices.

Phillips Carbon Black Limited: Proficiency, the Key

Phillips Carbon Black Limited (PCBL) takes the necessary steps for utilizing its resources efficiently. Its aim is to improve its business operations by aligning itself with the National Action Plan on Climate Change of the Government of India.

The company's environment, health and safety (EHS) policy provides the necessary guidance towards the conservation of the environment. It is determined for reducing carbon footprints. The company has a practice of recycling water and solid waste. In terms of environment and sustainability, the company has installed a facility for RWH from the existing building roof for reducing raw water consumption. It helps in providing stable supply of fresh water and, by doing so, most of the manufacturing units gets continuous water supply. Also, the process of recycling water through the effluent treatment plant (ETP) is also in place.

Maintaining the green environment around its plants in line with the EHS Policy, PCBL's co-generation power plants generate power from the tail gas of the carbon black process, thereby replacing the equal amount of fossil fuel fired by the plants. Plants have the goals of reducing the GHG emissions of CO_2 on an annual basis. The 12 MW co-generation power plant in Palej was the first unit in the world to be registered as a clean development mechanism (CDM) under the UNFCCC.

PCBL harnesses emitted waste gases while manufacturing carbon black for producing captive power for its plants as well as reuses treated wastewater in the production process. The company has also spearheaded the recycling of wastewater in its factories, thus making them zero-discharge facilities. In doing so, this process results in zero discharge of waste from its factories. More than 90 per cent of the solid waste generated is recycled internally across its facilities.

JEHANGIR RATANJI DADABHOY TATA AND THE CROSS PEN STORY

We Take Care of Things We Value

There is a story about Jehangir Ratanji Dadabhoy (JRD) Tata and his friend that proves the point. JRD had a friend who had a notorious habit of losing all his pens. Friends had more or less accepted his habit and would use very cheap pens so that he would not regret losing them. JRD gave a very radical suggestion to help the friend overcome the habit. He suggested his friend invest in the most expensive pen and see if this purchase would change him. As the story goes, the friend purchased a 22-carat gold Cross pen. JRD happened to meet his friend after a few months and enquired about his costly pen. The friend said that he had not lost his Cross pen. Since he had procured the pen, he had been very particular about how he was handling the pen. The simple story goes to show that people can change their attitude and behaviour about things they value. As the friend valued the pen, he took care of it and this principle is applicable to all the things that matter to us. If we value the environment and its preservation, we would be conscious of how our behaviour is affecting the environment. The lesson here is that if we want employees to adopt green ways, we have to make them value sustainability and resource usage optimization.[2]

ECONOMIC DEVELOPMENT

It refers to the development of the economy, which attempts to satisfy human needs and at the same time sustains natural resources and the environment for future generations. Greening

---

[2] https://www.speakingtree.in/blog/value-688884

of a workplace has the philosophy of enhancing profitability and marketability while reducing costs, increasing productivity, increasing shareholders' value and prioritizing green principles.

It focuses on creating an enterprise-friendly environment which may include the following:

1. Building resilient infrastructure that promotes sustainable industrialization that fosters green (or sustainable) innovation

2. Promoting just, peaceful and inclusive societies and revitalizing the global partnership for sustainable economic development

To extend it to the example of *Lemon Tree*, it was found that a lot of cost saving is done by having green practices in the hotel. In some of the hotels of *Lemon Tree*, electricity is produced by solar panels. In all hotels, wastewater is treated and used for irrigation purposes. In some of the hotels of *Lemon Tree*, the treated water is further recycled and an ozone application technique is used to remove foul smell and bacterial growth. Unlike other hotels of similar capacity in terms of rooms, *Lemon Tree's* energy requirement is only 500 KV instead of 1,200 KV. Moreover, *Lemon Tree* consumes 18,000 units in comparison to 35,000 units used by its competitors with similar capacity. This helps in reducing both fixed and variable costs. They track water usage, and water controls and meters are put in all places to compare the usage of water every month. They follow and track their energy and water consumption compared with global energy efficiency index, which is 2.12 kwh/m²/year, but with Lemon Tree it is between 1.7/1.9 kwh/m²/year and 2.12 kwh/m²/year.

To minimize the usage of water, the hotel purchases green fix-tures from companies such as jaguar, which makes it easier for it to consume less water. For example, instead of flush valves, it uses flush tanks that use 3–6 litres of water per flush instead of flush valves that consume 6–7 litres of water. In general, the earlier experience of the hotel, per guest per day of utilization was 6–7 flushes; thus, with the new intervention, total savings of water per guest got translated into almost 50 per day. The washbasin fittings and mixtures in the hotel can also be said to be green, which use 4 litres of water per day per person instead of 8 litres of water per day per guest in other hotels in general. The hotel had mostly removed bathtubs in its bathrooms, which need a lot of water. Rather they give their guests the shower cubicles.

Also, for day-to-day purposes, they use non-removable beds with no space from the ground tile to the bed; thus, there is no scope of dirt placed there. This helps them in less cleaning and maintenance as beds are not needed to be removed or displaced. Moreover, they use the interior in such a manner that the space is utilized for multiple purposes; thus, they save their space, cost and energy of their manpower. They use wood plate on the walls where the handle of the door gets a continuous touch, which helps them in less damage to the wall where, in general, because of constant touch, the wall gets damaged and thus needs more maintenance. Moreover, in rooms, instead of using false ceiling lights, they use bigger hanging lamps, so that with one lamp they get the light of four false ceiling bulbs.

MARUTI: CORE VALUES SERVE AS LIGHTHOUSE

Another interesting story that speaks about the green workplace is *Maruti Suzuki* that drives Indians to the greener tomorrow. The company understands that green technology is the necessity of the hour and strives hard to improve environmental performance by introducing special initiatives for minimizing carbon footprints in its manufacturing operations, products and supply chain. Maruti Suzuki, the leader of the automobile industry in India, also boasts of the largest manufacturing facilities in the country. Although both manufacturing facilities work at full capacity, the company ensures that this does not harm or damage the environment.

Maruti believes that investment in environment-friendly technologies is the core value of the organization. Moreover, these efforts bring good results in the medium to long term. Maruti Suzuki has the distinction of being the first automobile company in India to register a CDM project with the UNFCCC. Since manufacturing is the core aspect of the company, the company has maintained a special focus on this. The company has identified five focus areas for protection of environment and optimum utilization of resources, namely material use and weight reduction, energy conservation, water conservation, air emissions reduction and waste management.

Maruti has been meticulously committed towards reducing pressure on the environment, working collaboratively with its customers, suppliers and surrounding communities, and planning a controlled usage of natural resources.

The company has embarked on to improve its processes for the efficient use of resources. It has continued with its *one gram one component* programme to reduce material consumption through re-engineering and design modification of existing vehicles. With this programme in place, *Maruti* is aiming to reduce the overall raw material consumption. Not only this, *Maruti* has implemented a system to use the scrap generated from their press shops. The scrap generated in press and casting operations are sent to vendors who manufacture child parts or for use in their manufacturing of the relevant products. The company focuses on yielding improvement to conserve resources. The scope of this activity was extended from their traditional sheet metal to plastics, electrical and casting operations. In 2011–2012, 287 yield improvement proposals were implemented, resulting in a total savings of over 2,000 tonnes.

In any manufacturing plant, energy consumption is a major vertical for costs and carbon footprints. In *Maruti*, facilities run on captive power plants that use natural gas, clean and green fuel. The newly commissioned plant at Manesar has been designed to make maximum use of natural light, thereby reducing the need for artificial lighting in daytime. Specific to the plants, in Gurgaon, some specific steps have been taken, such as the installation of waste heat recovery boilers and steam turbine generators for generating power from waste at the Gurgaon plant.

Maruti has introduced a new-generation electro-deposition paint coating that operates at low voltage and consumes less energy in paint operations. Aerodynamic energy-efficient fibre-reinforced plastic blades have replaced standard blades at cooling towers for lower energy consumption. Also, the voltage in the shops has also been optimized for lighting and motor loads, and desiccant-type air dryers have been introduced to reduce energy consumption.

Maruti is taking the eco-friendly road to green logistics by the way of using railways for transporting finished cars. In the last five years, around 5 lakh cars have been transported all over the country through rail, offsetting over 4,000 tonnes of CO_2 emissions. The company is now using around 30 rakes for the transportation of its cars, of which more than half include flexi-deck auto-wagon rakes, especially designed by the company.

LEELA WITH NEW INITIATIVES

In the light of its commitment towards prevention of pollution and continual improvement in environmental performance, along with economic and social development, *Hotel Leela* takes measures and initiatives by controlling the impact of activities, products and services on the environment. All *Leela* hotels adhere to save 10 per cent on energy cost on a year-on-year basis, 'We recognized the importance of alternate power source and established wind mills in Karnataka. Incidentally, we are working on introducing solar power generation at our Bangalore hotel,' as per *Leela's* representative Sunil Relia, VP, engineering Hotel Leela. At the Hotel 'Leela Palaces' as per Mr Relia, 'We also have rainwater harvesting and auto flush for public urinals in place.'

He added further:

> Our hotels are designed and operated with zero waste-water discharge to reduce site disturbance, green area provided is 25 per cent more than the local norms and species selected are of native/adaptive nature to reduce water consumption. We have efficient rainwater harvesting (RWH) system to recharge site aquifer through recharge pits to reduce storm water run-off volumes post development and these pits are cleaned and maintained periodically.

SOCIAL DEVELOPMENT

It refers to a process of creating sustainable, successful places that promote the well-being of all individuals of an organization by understanding the needs of people about their lives and work. It combines the design of the physical realm with the design of the social world. It enables an infrastructure for supporting social and cultural life, social amenities, systems for citizen engagement and spaces for people and places, reducing unemployment and poverty in the country by providing job opportunities for people with disabilities.

EMPLOYEE SENSITIZATION AND GUEST PARTNERSHIP

It is seen as enhancing the productivity and retention of employees. Along with this, improved environmental awareness among employees also helps in the overall management of the concept in the day-to-day manner more effectively.

When employees are sensitized and aware of environmental harms, they will take greater responsibility of following policies supporting green workplace. This also helps in getting increased competitive advantages in the industry with green competencies and results.

'We have a "Green Team" comprising of head of the departments (HODs) that conceptualizes and implements innovative ideas to conserve energy and preserve the environment. Oberoi had planted trees and tree guards around the hotel and their maintenance and upkeep is also the responsibility of Oberoi,' said Bharma. A comprehensive energy audit was carried out in late 2008 by a professional company for the property and their recommendations to reduce energy consumption were duly implemented.

The best practice by the *Oberoi* towards *guest engagement and partnership* with guests is *engaging guests in conservation efforts that can work quite well*. Room linen is not changed on a daily basis in case a guest stays for more than one night, but when guest specifically requests for linen change, only on the second day the linen is changed. Moreover, for the efficient use of the energy used for lighting and temperature, they are controlled by the guest as per their moods and requirements. Unnecessarily, the room is not set to low temperature and the lights get dim in case there is not much requirement of lighting. 'Following certain norms and strictures right from construction stages also helps in conservation in the long run,' says Bharma.

Delta Hotels and Resorts programme by *Marriott* is the approach of engaging guests in the environment and sustainability-related initiative. The hotel has the partnership with WEarth. The two combined give an opportunity to the guest that virtually they can plant a tree. Under this, guest will plant a tree for each night they have stayed in the hotel. The WEarth plants the actual trees on behalf of their guests. This exercise actually is called *Green STAY*, which helps in reforestation efforts. Guests also feel that they have really done something towards the environment and thus feel satisfied. The other benefit they get is when they re-book the same hotel, they get the opportunity of seeing the actual plant roped by them. This ultimately gives a lot of satisfaction.

Marriott has a partnership with the International Union for Conservation of Nature. The mangroves restoration effort is for the great cause. This is for the support of coastal communities in Thailand. Mangrove trees have been planted across Thailand. When guests stay in these hotels, funds are raised from them for supporting mangroves and replanting at degraded coastal sites around Thailand.

> *A Chinese proverb says that the longest journey begins with a single step.*

There are plenty of business houses that are striving to go for a greener workplace. Some organizations are working towards achievement of targets, while others are just pondering on green thoughts and moving on. Many small actions/initiatives can collectively make a huge impact on the organization's sustainability efforts.

A number of organizations are aware of the environmental consequences of their functioning, thus making concerted efforts towards reducing the negative environmental impact as caused by their industrial behaviour. Many organizations have transformed the workplace into a green workplace to align with the vision and mission of the organization that advocates greening or environmental consciousness.

These stories elucidate that if there is a will and realization towards the environment, and we really want to live and leave for the future generation in a liveable condition, steps towards these directions are must. The baby steps can transform an ordinary place into a green place or a more sustainable place. Even the small intervention taken by us can change the entire story of pollution and GHG emissions towards a better place with better living conditions.

The aforementioned examples show that the practices followed by companies are a real example of green initiatives. For example, an 80-year-old building can a become LEED certified gold-rated building. The carbon black company PCBL and Maruti Suzuki are registered under the UNFCCC. Maruti Suzuki had started following green measures even before the Environment (Protection) Act, 1986, came into force in India. In the hospitality sector, ITC Hotels sets an example of how the environment and sustainability can be achieved while leading in business and profitability. Lemon Tree is an example that can serve as a role model to low- and mid-segment players in hospitality sector, as with innovative efforts sustainability goals can be achieved even though the company is not in the five-star category. Another example that Leela and Oberoi hotels have given is also worth appreciating. Thus, it can be concluded that where there is a will there is a way.

Let us just take a green ride here to some of the pioneers towards *greening*.

One good turn deserves another.

SUGGESTED READINGS

Hotel Leelaventure Limited. (2019). The Leela. https://www.bseindia.com/bseplus/annualreport/500193/5001930319.pdf

Kasera, S. (2019). Annual Report 2018–19. https://www.pcblltd.com/download/annual-report-2018-19/

Lemon Tree Hotels Limited. (2019). Annual Report 2018–19. https://www.lemontreehotels.com/factsheet/Policies/LTHL AnnualReport2018-19.pdf

Maruti Suzuki. (2019). Integrated report 2018–19. https://marutistoragenew.blob.core.windows.net/msilintiwebpdf/Integrated_Report_2018_19_Low.pdf

https://www.greenhotelier.org/destinations/asia-pacific/itc-hotels-sustains-its-sustainability-credentials/

https://www.itchotels.in/content/dam/projects/hotelswebsite/itc-hotels/luxury-collection/Environment/ITC GREEN.pdf

https://www.cesc.co.in/?page_id=1980

https://www.cesc.co.in/?page_id=226

https://www.cesc.co.in/?cat=16

https://www.pcblltd.com/pcbl-sustainability-review-2018/

https://www.marutisuzuki.com/corporate/about-us/sustainability

https://esgrobot.com/maruti-suzuki-sustainability-report/

https://www.eihltd.com/investor_relations/annual_reports.asp

https://www.lemontreehotels.com/factsheet/LTH_CSR_Policy.pdf

LEADERS' CORNER

Industries all over the world are expected to take a more active role in promoting sustainability. In the past few decades, there has been a rise in the number of initiatives on environmental sustainability taken at both macro and micro levels. During the UN's Climate Summit in New York held in September 2019, there was a clarion call to the attending heads of organizations to demonstrate leadership initiatives on climate change. Majority of the companies participating in the summit accepted the target of zero emissions by 2050. This act will help to counter the threat of rise in global temperatures by 1.5 °C as predicted by environmental scientists. There have been similar summits and conferences in which the seriousness of the global threat has been discussed at length. The message seems to be sinking in as many organizations are stepping up to deal with this global phenomenon. If surveys and media reports are any proof to go by, CEOs worldwide are treating the goals of carbon neutrality and sustainability as their topmost priority.[1]

---

[1] https://www.cnbc.com/2020/01/21/davos-climate-changeand-ceos.html

THE CRUSADERS OF SUSTAINABILITY AGENDA

At the micro level, we find lone crusaders who have been pursuing the sustainability agenda not only in their organizations but also have taken it upon themselves to spread environmental awareness all over the world. One such person is Yvon Chouinard, the founder and chairman of Patagonia.[2] Patagonia, a sports and outdoor clothes brand, has firmly established itself as a sustainable brand. The UN presented the Champions of the Earth award to Patagonia in 2019.

Yvon Chouinard is very passionate about the environmental cause, he changed the mission statement of his organization to 'Patagonia is in business to save our home planet,' which clearly signalled the broad intent and scope of the organization's commitment to sustainability, and this had an impact on all the people associated with the organization. The organization is determined to replace fossil fuels with renewable sources completely by 2025. They are investing in organic fibre and also convincing supply chain partners to become sustainable by reducing carbon footprints. He has encouraged Indian farmers to grow organic cotton and use natural ways in agriculture by paying a premium for their environment-friendly produce. The company also suggested its Japanese supplier to change to green energy. Beside this, Chouinard has produced a number of environmental documentaries meant to highlight some serious environmental issues. The sustainability story of Patagonia has only been made possible due to the unwavering commitment and efforts of the founder, who not only imbued the entire organization and its ecosystem with sustainability but also raised environmental conservation issues on international fora. He calls himself a 'pessimist', somebody who believes the world is doomed, and is highly critical of the efforts of some of

[2] https://www.fastcompany.com/90280950/exclusive-patagoniais-in-business-to-save-our-home-planet

the global leaders who are investing in space expeditions. His point of view is very simple and practical—why look for other abodes when it is possible to save our own planet.

Patagonia's story reflects the deep conviction of Mr Yvon Chouinard that made his organization so environmentally conscious and his commitment to spread awareness at the global level. Being a self-acknowledged pessimist, he thinks that his efforts are not enough to deal with the colossal magnitude of environmental degradation, but that does not deter him from taking new initiatives.

It is well established that leaders are the initiators of big changes in organizations. Once business leaders start looking within and introspect on how their businesses are impacting the environment, it becomes the first step in lessening environmental harm. Leaders understand that such actions not only help them to demonstrate their social and environmental responsibilities but are good for the business. An example of this is Larry Fink, the founder and CEO of BlackRock, a global investment management company, who at the beginning of 2020 wrote a letter to the CEOs emphasizing the importance of sustainability in investment decisions. He called climate risk an investment risk and expressed his intention to consider sustainability in the decision-making criterion. In the letter to clients, he announced a number of initiatives: *making sustainability integral to portfolio construction and risk management; exiting investments that present a high sustainability-related risk, such as thermal coal producers; launching new investment products that screen fossil fuels; and strengthening our commitment to sustainability and transparency in our investment stewardship activities.*[3]

Similarly, the CEO and Chairman of Schneider Electric, Jean-Pascal Tricoire, concurred that sustainable business models

---

[3] https://www.blackrock.com/corporate/investor-relations/larry-fink-ceo-letter

make economic sense; for example, carbon discharges primarily are an indicator of the organization's inefficiencies. Hence, reductions would imply enhanced efficiencies and improved revenue streams. As pointed out by him, stakeholders can be the drivers of the sustainability movement. As there is an increasing awareness on environmental matters among the youth, who comprise customer as well as talent group for organizations, it is expected that they will want to engage with organizations that share a similar concern for the environment.

These ideas have found resonance in the Accenture/UN Global Compact CEO study[4] 2019, in which the leaders surveyed acknowledged awareness about synergies between business and social impact. Two-thirds of the CEOs accepted that businesses were trying to work on global issues, and a large majority of them suggested that such efforts would positively benefit the future prospects of their business. The primary lever for sustainable actions were the customer's expectations, the organization's brand, trust quotient and the reputation of the organization.

LEADERS NEED TO VIEW SUSTAINABILITY AS TOP AGENDA

On the contrary, a survey conducted by PwC, which gathered responses from 3,501 CEOs in 83 territories of the USA in 2019, revealed that 'climate change and environmental damage' were not high priorities for CEOs, who ranked this matter at number 11 in terms of threat to growth opportunities for organizations. Interestingly, CEOs viewed climate change-related matters as an opportunity. The survey results are an indicator that sustainability movement is still not as strong as it should be. The respondents claimed that environmental initiatives in supply chain management and the production

---

[4] https://www.accenture.com/us-en/insights/strategy/ungcceostudy

process would give them an edge in the market as stakeholders and customers look into the environmental criteria in their decision making. According to them, as employee activism is gaining currency, prospective employees are positively preferring green employers. It can be implied that though there is growing awareness in business leadership about environmental stewardship, there is a need for higher commitment for further action.

The contradiction between environmental beliefs and actions affect the pace at which organizations are adopting sustainability. The values, beliefs, behaviours and messages of top leadership set the direction for the organization's future. The sustainability initiative of organizations cannot kick-start until the leaders totally commit to the environmental cause. Support from the top management team is very important. For a long time, organizations refrained from taking up sustainability initiatives because leaders believed that this was an expensive proposition. If the leaders wish to promote sustainability in the organization, they need to walk the talk. They need to begin right at the beginning with revisions in their mission, vision and shared values, and operational goals which need to be infused with sustainability. This was made very clear by Alan Jope, CEO of Unilever, when allegations about less than 1 per cent use of recycled material in packaging were levelled against the organization. While addressing the One Young World Conference, he said:

> Push us, call us out when we don't do a good enough job. We are in the news for not taking enough action on plastic through last year and it's true and I feel bad about that, but boy are we going to move quickly in the next two years. You watch us and judge us by our actions not by our words.[5]

---

[5] https://phvntom.com/unilever-ceo-tells-activists-to-call-usout-amid-plastic-criticism/

In another interesting communication, Jope shared his controversial views on plastics. He mentioned *that it was a wonderful material that was safe and helped in reducing food waste. It is better in terms of reducing carbon footprint than aluminium or glass.*

This viewpoint was also shared by the heads of other fast-moving consumer goods companies like Coca-Cola. Jope's suggestion on climate change was shifting from the linear 'take, use, throw' model to a fully circular economy by drastically reducing the usage of virgin plastic. He supported the view that plastics should be retained in the economy. The belief system of top leadership has a huge impact on the sustainability strategy of organizations and leaders with a strong environmental consciousness have worked to make organizations sustainable.

One of the most important steps towards leadership in embracing sustainability is to assess and acknowledge the impact of businesses on the environment, people, communities and stakeholders. It is important to understand the scope for sustainability as well as the environmental impacts on all aspects of business.

Do you know which companies are among the 100 most sustainable companies in the world in 2020?

Read more at https://www.forbes.com/sites/samanthatodd/2020/01/21/who-are-the-100-most-sustainable-companies-of-2020/#3099379314a4

CHALLENGES LEADERS FACE

The engagement of stakeholders is one of the key challenges that leaders need to tackle when it comes to incorporating the sustainability agenda into business (Crews, 2010). The engagement of stakeholders in itself presents a unique set of challenges. For instance, all stakeholders need to be committed to the cause for getting macro-level environmental outcomes. Alan Jope made an interesting observation: *We need business, government, civil society and citizens to come together to represent the change that we need.*

The problem with stakeholder engagement can occur when the interests of all stakeholders cannot be met at the same time and there are potential trade-offs. One example of this could be the premium customers who are expected to pay for green products. Very often, in certain markets and geographies, customers may be too price sensitive and unwilling to shell out more money for green products or brands. Similarly, Nike has often faced a lot of criticism for outsourcing production work in Asian countries where child labour was employed by the partner organization and the partners were found guilty of making people work in sweatshop-like environments. Nike, though not directly responsible for such unethical practices, had to own up to its partners' actions. Similarly, the BP oil spill in the Gulf of Mexico, where 130 million gallons of crude oil got spilt into the sea, led to the massive destruction of marine birds and animals, causing BP to receive a lot of flak. According to a Business Insider Report (2009),[6] majority of the 15 worst sustainability companies around the world were energy companies. BP's accident has been termed as an environmental disaster of the worst kind. The mishandling of the crisis and the lack of taking ownership made BP lose some its most loyal and significant customers.[7]

---

[6] https://www.businessinsider.com/the-15-worst-companies-for-the-environment-2009-9?IR=T
[7] http://www.experian.com/blogs/marketing-forward/2010/08/11/bp-customer-base-falls-in-wake-of-spill/; https://www.independent.co.uk/environment/deepwaterhorizon-oil-spill-gulf-mexico-fish-pollution-a9466761.html

A UNIQUE EXAMPLE OF SUSTAINABLE LEADERSHIP

Another example of sustainable leadership can be found in Interface, an Atlanta-based organization. The carpet-making company has recently changed its mission from 'Mission Zero' to 'Climate Take Back'.

The bold mission reads as follows: *To be the first company that, by its deeds, shows the entire industrial world what sustainability is in all its dimensions: People, process, product, place and profits— by 2020—and in doing so we will become restorative through the power of influence.*

The company has set out to remove all kinds of adverse environmental impacts from its operations by 2020. It wishes to have nil wastage, no GHG emissions and less water consumption. It aspires to promote a circular economy by promoting product take back and usage of recycled or organic material as well as greening the supply chain and paying attention to the welfare of stakeholders. As a part of its commitment, it wishes to make four commitments, which are as follows:

- We will bring carbon home and reverse climate change.

- We will create supply chains that benefit all life.

- We will make factories like forests.

- We will transform dispersed materials into products and goodness.

The credit for making the organization environmentally sustainable goes to founder, Ray Anderson. He gave a serious thought to the environmental implications of his work when he was questioned about the environmental impacts of the organization's work, and he did not have an answer. Paul Hawken's book *The Ecology of Commerce* made him realize that he was 'a plunderer of the earth'.

This realization laid the groundwork for the company to take on an environmentally sustainable role and focus on future restoration. Interface became the front runner in the sustainability movement in its industry and, as the first mover, was ridiculed and expected to be doomed for its focus on its sustainability practices.

Thus, it is seen that the clarion call has to come from the leader who is at the helm of affairs. The leader can take a bird's eye view of the company and decide as to where it is headed. The leader also needs to believe that no effort is small. Ray Anderson called his sustainability journey ascending 'Mount Sustainability', and the company continued its sustainability journey in spite of the economic slowdown and steep rise in petroleum products. Sustainability was deeply ingrained in the cultural fabric of the company. Interface was recycling used carpets to make new products, and the sourcing cost was more than the cost of sourcing virgin nylon. In spite of the economy not doing well, Interface managed to get business as it had earned enough goodwill in the market.

Do you know the top leaders who have played a crucial role in promoting sustainability?

Read more at https://www.forbes.com/sites/solitairetownsend/2018/07/18/46-sustainability-leaders-who-are-also-women/#5c81351d1110

MAINTAINING A LEADER'S SUSTAINABILITY LEGACY

After the death of the founder who spearheaded the sustainability movement, the company lost its focus on sustainability and had very lacklustre performance in the subsequent years. Interface, in the initial years, started a Dream Team which comprised experts and allies who supported Interface in its sustainability initiative. But over the years, the impact of these initiatives wore off and sustainable actions, which had earlier provided a competitive advantage, now became generic practices in the industry. The new CEO, faced with the challenge of reviving the entire sustainability movement, began by regrouping the dream team. The focus was now not only on zero environmental footprints but also to achieve a positive impact on the environment.

The sustainability perspective has also led the company break new grounds in innovation and environment conservation. In 2012, it introduced Net-Works, which were nylon carpets made of discarded and recycled fishing nets. The nets were sourced from the Philippines and Interface recycled 100 tonnes of fishing net wastes. As Jo Ann Herold, former chief marketing officer of Interface, once observed: *What was remarkable was the company's commitment to sustainability, which was reflected in all its actions and found resonance in all kinds of narratives ranging from innovation to investments.*

Under the leadership of current CEO Hendrix, the company's mission has transcended traditional sustainability which implies the reversing of the effects of climate change by 'bringing carbon home'. According to him, carbon was harmful in the gaseous form but had huge benefits when it blended with the earth in solid form. So he initiated the idea of using carbon for building things. In fact, Interface has taken sustainability to new heights by designing what they call 'forest factories', that is, setting up factories in the midst of the forest without disrupting the natural ecosystem in any way.

If we were to identify the qualities that promote sustainable leadership, they could be very diverse. Although it definitely begins with the leader being absolutely passionate about the environment and willing to embark upon the sustainability journey, there are other qualities too that can lead to success. Tideman et al. (2013) have discussed six elements of sustainable leadership that are imperative for sustainable organizations.

Sustainable Leadership Elements	Business Implication
Context	Recognizing interdependence; complexity; ambiguity; interconnectedness; resource constraint; regulators and mega-trends
Consciousness	Mindsets; world views; beliefs; mental models and attitudes
Continuity	Long-term horizon; courage; strength; common purpose; centeredness and change processes
Connectedness	Serving needs of all stakeholders; both long- and short-term influencing; collaboration; trust; fairness; altruism; relatedness and needs instead of wants

(Continued)

(Continued)

Sustainable Leadership Elements	Business Implication
Creativity	Innovation for sustainable shared value creation; sustainable business models; new value measurement models and flow
Collectiveness	Scaling up for collective impact; embedding sustainability in business structures and sustainable consumption

Source: Tideman et al. (2013).

WHAT LEADERS NEED TO DO

Believe in the Impact

Leaders need to believe that sustainability is a source of competitive advantage and, in order to blend commercial value with environmental good, leaders need to see the broader context in which the business is to make an impact. The context in which sustainability is to be implemented is crucial. Epstein et al. (2010) have discussed the influencers of a successful sustainability model that include the external context (regulatory and geographical), the internal context (mission, corporate strategy, corporate organizational structure, organizational culture and systems), the business context (industry sector, customers and products), and human and financial resources. Leaders need to have a perfect understanding of interrelationships among these influencers. The leader also needs to have knowledge of the interdependence that business has with the community and the environment and how the business makes an impact in the short and long term.

When employees know that the top leadership believes in sustainability, they would be assured of top leadership support.

Sustainability efforts would never be successful if the leader is not convinced of its merits.

Create a Sustainability Culture

Another important task for leaders is to create a culture that promotes sustainability. Leaders are important influencers who shape the organization's culture. The sustainability culture needs to be supported by organization-wide green operational systems and practices. Leaders also need to comprehend and understand sustainability and its implications both inside and outside the organization.

Champion the Green Movement in the Organization

Leaders can promote sustainability only when they believe that sustainability is imperative for the organization. They need to relentlessly communicate how important environmental consideration is for the organization, include the environmental intent in the company's messages to all stakeholders, institute environmental impact criteria in the organizational decision-making process, for example, not sourcing material from vendors who are not green, approving product designs that are environmentally conducive and being transparent in reporting sustainability performance to all. Once the leader starts shouting about the importance of sustainability from the rooftops, it becomes easier to gather the troops to take on the sustainability challenge.

Change Values

The leader also needs to have a pro-social value system that transcends the values of commercial gains and business interest.

The narratives shared in the chapter earlier demonstrate that leaders were evolved and wanted to make their businesses examples of responsible and eco-friendly management. This was very much reflected in the Yvon Chouinard's narrative, as he not only looked at his organization but also at how the entire ecosystem needed to change for a better EM. To quote Paul Polman, CEO of Unilever:

> Most businesses operate and say how can I use society and the environment to be successful? We are saying the opposite—how can we contribute to the society and the environment to be successful? So it starts with asking the right question to yourself, which will change the way you think.[8]

When analysing styles of leadership that would suit sustainable organizations, researchers identified transformational leadership, responsible, authentic and ethical leadership to be enablers of sustainability in organizations. One of the things which is common to most of them is the attribute of consciousness in the leader that makes the environmental cause believable to the followers.

Have Courage

The courage to start the mammoth exercise of making the organization green, to convince everybody, including stakeholders, can be demanding and can have setbacks just like any other change initiative. The leader has to make sure that the initiatives are well

---

[8] https://www.forumforthefuture.org/blog/paul-polman-role-model-for-today-and-tomorrow

executed and, instead of employing a fragmented approach to sustainability, leaders need to go beyond statutory requirements, delve in ambitious, high- impact initiatives and ensure continuity of the same.

Be a Mentor

The leader needs to guide and teach others how to factor in sustainability in routine operations. In some instances, it is said that leaders need to be passionate about sustainability and ensure that it integrates with all that an organization does. A leader's passion and profound commitment would help in creating a culture that supports sustainability.

Be the Architect

The leader has to be the architect who will help to develop a sustainability-related business model in which the vision and mission are sustainability inclusive and the organization's structure, culture and HR practices all support the sustainability agenda.

Acknowledge and Address

In a number of situations, there are trade-offs involved in implementing sustainability-related initiatives. Leaders need to manage several paradoxes such as short-term versus long-term orientation, profits versus social impacts and at the same time take everyone along the journey. Sustainability is not about one person's initiative, it needs to be adopted by everyone to make the entire organization sustainable. Efforts need to have a dual focus—short-term micro initiatives as well as long-term impactful projects. Leaders have to acknowledge how being green helps to meet the varied needs of diverse stakeholder groups that are becoming environmentally conscious.

Encourage Creativity

There is also a need to encourage creativity in the kind of initiatives that need to be taken. It should be more than having routine EMSs in order to make a difference. Leaders need to engage in a lot of out-of-the-box thinking to ideate new sustainability-driven projects. The Net-Works of Interface was a very innovative solution to a sustainability issue.

Build Strong Foundation

Institutionalizing sustainability rather than embarking on it as a temporary assignment is important. The leader needs to keep building on previous initiatives and to integrate sustainability into the organization's mission, strategy, structure and culture.

Make a Bigger Impact

Sustainable leadership may extend beyond the boundaries of the organization to include stakeholders, for example, taking responsibility for the greening of the supply chain, taking on environmentally responsible corporate social responsibility (CSR) actions to support the greening of the adjoining community, participating in business forums, world forums that deliberate upon the future of the environment and the role of business in it.

CREATING A BALANCE

There are many awards that honour leaders who have guided organizations to walk the green path. According to the founders of one such prestigious award, Matt Harney, SEAL Awards' Founder:

> Companies, CEOs and corporate boards have a simple but not easy choice before them: whether to exhibit real leadership by investing in sustainable business practices. The sustainability leaders—like our SEAL Award recipients—can secure lasting legacies for their grandchildren and corporate stakeholders alike; ESG leaders will have reputations and balance sheets that survive the climate crisis.

It is a difficult journey for a sustainable leader to create a balance between commercial and environmental needs. But leaders have done that in the past and continue doing so, by leaving behind a powerful legacy and setting an example for the next generation of leaders. Such leaders emerge as they realize that there is a very deep business environment to connect and this sacred connection needs to be honoured.

Let's Reflect

What changes in your style of leadership would you like to make after reading this chapter?

A._____

B._____

C._____

D._____

E._____

REFERENCES

Crews, D. E. (2010). Strategies for implementing sustainability: Five leadership challenges. *SAM Advanced Management Journal*, *75*(2), 15.

Epstein, M. J., Buhovac, A. R., & Yuthas, K. (2010). Implementing sustainability: The role of leadership and organizational culture. *Strategic Finance*, *91*(10), 41.

Tideman, S. G., Arts, M. C., & Zandee, D. P. (2013). Sustainable leadership: Towards a workable definition. *Journal of Corporate Citizenship*, *49*(3), 17–33.

SUGGESTED READINGS

Baumgartner, R. J. (2009). Organizational culture and leadership: Preconditions for the development of a sustainable corporation. *Sustainable Development*, *17*(2), 102–113.

Galpin, T., Whitttington, J. L., & Bell, G. (2015). Is your sustainability strategy sustainable? Creating a culture of sustainability. *Corporate Governance*, *15*(1), 1–17.

Hargreaves, A., & Fink, D. (2012). *Sustainable leadership* (Vol. 6). John Wiley & Sons.

Metcalf, L., & Benn, S. (2013). Leadership for sustainability: An evolution of leadership ability. *Journal of Business Ethics*, *112*(3), 369–384.

Porter, T. H., Gallagher, V. C., & Lawong, D. (2016). The greening of organizational culture: Revisited fifteen years later. *American Journal of Business*, *31*(4), 206–226.

https://www.greenbiz.com/article/expanding-role-sustainability-leadership

https://www.greenbiz.com/article/governance-unexplored-secret-behind-patagonias-business-success

https://www.businessinsider.com/the-15-worst-companies-for-the-environment-2009-9?IR=T

ENCOURAGING GREEN HR PRACTICES

Sustainability[1] and greening of organizations have become important buzzwords in recent times, but there are organizations that have been pioneers of the sustainability movement. They have for a long time balanced the environmental and profit imperatives. One such organization that deserves special mention is 3M, a company that manufactures a diverse array of products such as adhesives, abrasives, laminates, electrical and electronic connecting and insulating materials. 3M has been rated as one of the most innovative organizations in the world, as it has also ensured that sustainability is always on its agenda. As early as in the 1970s, it resolved to look into the environmental issues caused by its operations and handle pollution at its point of origin. 3M decided to innovate products that would cause the least environmental harm, and act on the conservation of natural resources, besides adhering to the environmental legislation and formalities. 3M believed in and acted on the philosophy of 3P, which is an acronym for

---

[1] Some of the data shared in this chapter are based on the interviews conducted while writing the book with HR professionals from eminent companies well known for their sustainability efforts.

pollution prevention pays, by changing product compositions, processes and recycling of materials. Over the next two decades, organizations such as Novartis, Chevron, Dow, International Business Machines (IBM) and Monsanto began addressing the environmental aspect by reconfiguring designs, production set-up and processes to reduce the environmental footprints of their operations. It can be noted that good companies had begun taking the sustainability agenda seriously from early on and were setting examples for other organizations to follow by busting the myth that incorporating sustainability adds to costs and chips away at the bottom line.

Let us look at some of the good green practices that are worth emulating.

REPORTING ON SUSTAINABLE ACTIONS

Times have changed, and in today's world most of the organizations have varying degrees of environmental orientation. As stakeholders have become environmentally aware and demanding, organizations are disseminating information about their sustainability initiatives on all forums. The annual reports of companies, the voluntary sharing of sustainability reports prepared in conformity with the Global Reporting Initiative (GRI) framework, have become the reporting norms all over the world. The websites of organizations have a separate section devoted to outlining their sustainability goals and actions. Thus, reporting on sustainability initiatives has become a good practice which most of the environmentally responsible organizations follow. Reporting helps organizations set an example in the industry and make other players follow the same. This also serves as a motivating factor for internal stakeholders, as there is a sense of pride in being associated with an organization that believes in sustainability.

ALIGNING HR PRACTICES WITH SUSTAINABILITY STRATEGY

Another set of practices that can help organizations to become green would be the greening of HR processes. If HR managers can integrate the sustainability strategy with the employee life cycle, it can give tremendous boost to the environmental initiatives of the organization.

Green Employer Value Proposition

When organizations represent themselves as green, they enhance their value proposition. This green image becomes useful in attracting candidates who are environmentally conscious and would like to work for green organizations (Behrend, Baker & Thompson, 2009). Many companies, such as IBM, General Motors and Microsoft, have added sustainability-related information in their recruitment messages. Studies have corroborated that students who are prospective employees pay attention to the environmental and social contribution of the organizations they would like to work for. The websites of most of the Fortune 500 companies provide information on their environmental focus and contributions. Targeting prospective employees with green attitudes and competencies makes it easier for organizations to promote green practices and pro-environmental behaviour in organizations once these individuals join the organization.

Green Key Result Areas

Organization are including green criteria in job descriptions and key result areas (KRAs) for jobs that have an environmental dimension. This was corroborated by senior managers of organizations such as PCBL, Maruti Suzuki Ltd and CESC which were included in a study conducted by the authors on sustainability. In the case of Maruti Suzuki Ltd., along with technical KPIs, there are some KPIs that measure how efficient resource utilization and resource savings are. Employees who have scored high on environmental KPIs are given recognition and rewards. Such organizations, even at the time of recruitment, give importance to candidates who have initiated and executed environmental projects in their career in the form of designing/redesigning products that required less resources or helped reduce waste of resources at the workplace. In Maruti Suzuki Ltd., at the time of recruitment, they look for candidates who have technical competence and would adapt well to the culture of sustainability.

Do you know what kind of mistakes organizations make when they go paperless?

Read more at https://www.laserfiche.com/ecmblog/4-big-mistakes-organizations-make-when-going-paperless/

Employee Initiatives

Organizations that have made greening a priority expect environment-centric behaviour from their people, such behaviour would centre around judicious utilization of resources, assessment of environmental impact in decision-making, recycling and repurposing of resources, and adoption of renewable energy sources. Most organizations run sustainability-linked employee suggestion schemes. Maruti Suzuki Ltd., PCBL and CESC run successful suggestion schemes for shop floor employees, which have led to a lot of savings in energy and resource consumption.

Environmental Training

Another area in which organizations focus in order to encourage green orientation among employees is to provide them environmental training that focuses on environmental aware-ness and adoption of green practices. In recent times, the hospitality industry has taken its environmental responsibility very seriously and has initiated a number of steps to cut down the consumption of resources. Ms Aradhana Lal, VP Brand, Communications and Sustainability Initiatives from the Lemon Tree Group of hotels, mentioned how employees are made to undergo a series of training sessions that focus on the environ-ment. Employees are supposed to follow environment-friendly practices while serving their guests. Guests receive messages on conservation of water. Among some of the practices to con-serve water, the hotel follows a practice of serving only half a glass of water in restaurants, and guests are requested to ask for replenishment. Besides this, guests are subtly discouraged from requesting for change of linen in their rooms. These measures may seem trivial but, collectively, they make a huge difference in reducing the consumption of water. Employees need to learn and follow these practices and politely encourage guests to reduce the wastage of resources.

Research has demonstrated how environmental training can positively influence EMS in organizations (Sammalisto & Brorson, 2008). The current Gen Y is believed to get motivated by meaningful work and the organization's environmental con-sideration adds a meaningful perspective to their jobs (Nohria, Groysberg & Lee, 2008). There is evidence that suggests that encouraging green practices can enhance employee satisfac-tion, motivation, engagement and retention. According to Mr Tanmay, an HR professional from Jockey India:

> Every sector has bodies that give accreditation, recog-nition for compliance with rules and processes that are not easy for everyone to comply with. It gives a sense of pride and accomplishment that you have done some-thing and you have done it indirectly to benefit society.

The organization's overall image improves and the gains are intangible and have indirect benefits. There is no direct correlation between employee satisfaction and retention but it acts as an enabler.

Making Sustainability a Part of Everyday Routine

According to Mr Sidharth Balakrishna, Principal, cKinetics and former Group Head of Strategy and Innovation, Essel (Zee) Group, who has considerable experience in the oil industry, mentioned that there is scope to have a number of small projects that can have a payback time of 6–9 months in areas of resource conservation, but the problem in some organizations is that such projects are not included among the day-to-day initiatives. But there is scope to make EM part of the organization's routines in which employees consciously take actions to save resources. In many organizations, employees are encouraged to follow simple daily environment-friendly practices such as follows:

1. Reducing printouts to a bare minimum

2. Encouraging double-sided printing

3. Switching off the lights and air conditioner (AC) when leaving office

4. Car-pooling to reduce carbon footprints

5. Curbing travel to other locations through the use of communication technologies

Small Actions Go a Long Way

These simple practices can make a big difference in reducing energy bills and paper consumption in organizations. Another very interesting change has been the substitution of trophies, mementoes made of metal and glass with green saplings in corporate gifting practices.

Another good example of an organization actively involved in environment management is Wipro which runs a very active Water Stewardship programme in which they focus on enhancing water efficiency by reducing the use of fresh water per employee, attempt to obtain water from adjoining communities in a responsible manner, especially in areas where availability of water is a problem, view access to water resource as a business risk and factor that in their plans for the future. Miss Rituparna Ghosh, senior HR leader from Wipro, in her interaction with the authors mentioned how Wipro has set water conservation goals for improving water efficiency by cutting freshwater use per employee by 5 per cent on a year-on-year basis and reducing absolute water consumption in existing campuses by 20 per cent between FY2016 and FY2021.

Examples of several companies show that encouraging employees to participate in environmental programmes and eco-initiatives helps organizations further their sustainability initiatives.

Hindustan Computers Limited

Hindustan Computers Limited (HCL) has always believed in greening its processes and making 'go green' an enterprise-wide initiative.[2] It has instituted an 'Internal Waste Management System' that ensures the recycling of waste generated in manufacturing processes. As a part of its eco-initiatives, it encourages employees to plant trees. It takes care of the environment inside the office by ensuring good quality of water and air, and curbs travelling outside to minimum. Employees

---

[2] https://www.academia.edu/10479594/Green_HRM_An_Innovative_Approach_to_Environmental_Sustainability

are encouraged to generate ideas and take initiatives on environmental conservation. Employees organize an annual earth hour and this event involves reducing lighting in offices and homes, and contributing ideas to minimize resource usage. The organization encourages employees to form eco-councils which function in consultation with the functional departments and work on environmental actions. It is seen that CSR and sustainability-linked initiatives can serve as important employee engagement tools as they provide employees with opportunities to think beyond the routine concerns of the organization and to give back to society and nature. Employees at HCL feel much more engaged when they participate in different forums and groups that work towards the betterment of the organization and the environment.

Phillips Carbon Black Ltd

At PCBL, all green initiatives have been made possible because of the involvement of employees. The company's creation of different teams at the plant level is meant to involve employees in the organization's sustainability initiatives.

There are focus improvement projects (FIPs) that operate under the motto of 'go green'. Project members participate in formal brainstorming sessions to get new ideas. The teams are headed by the Plant Head and the Manufacturing Excellence Head. Plants have five daily management teams (DMTs) which conduct morning meetings and field meetings. Management team meetings are held at different locations to identify abnormalities in operations and consist of technical staff, workers and contractual staff who regularly and deliberately work upon improvement opportunities and ideas to make work easy and bring overall benefits to the company. Reviews are also held every Saturday by the plant head with the site manufacturing coordinator and the DMT/FIP team in order to encourage focused participation.

It is seen that employees are systematically allowed to be part of only two teams at a time and that in review meetings any member from the team can be picked up to report on the progress of activities facilitating deeper engagement among employees. To instil better awareness of environmental issues and recent developments in EM, employees are sent to other plants to learn and assimilate their best practices. The company has sent 3–4 employees to visit AkzoNobel, ranked no. 1, in the Dow Jones Sustainability Index, to learn from their safety, health and environment practices.

It is often said that a little appreciation goes a long way. As part of its employee recognition programme, named Sampark, the company has given rewards to 350 employees out of the 400 who were nominated for their contribution to the environment. There are localized reward and recognition systems as well. In Kerala plants, there are cash prizes, in Palej employees are honoured with Greentech Environment Awards in the gold category and, as a result of these initiatives, the company has witnessed a considerable reduction in environmental complaints in its different facilities. One major success for the company is the embedding of environmental and safety consciousness among all employees. Employees take pride in managing the environment which was missing earlier. The twin challenges that the company faces on an ongoing basis are keeping up with technological changes that support the environment and maintaining and strengthening a culture that values environmental consciousness.

GREEN INFRASTRUCTURE

Another interesting way in which organizations have encouraged green is by recalibrating their buildings into green buildings. As per the definition given by the World Green Building Council, 'A "green" building is a building that, in its design, construction or operation, reduces or eliminates negative impacts, and can create positive impacts, on our climate and natural environment.' As tabulated in the website of the World Green Building Council, the features that need to be included to turn a building into green are as follows:

> efficient use of resources, focus on renewable sources of energy for example solar energy, minimization of redundancies and wastes, recycling and repurposing of waste, use of sustainable material in construction, maintenance of indoor air quality, building design based on environmental consideration and a design that is scalable and adaptable to suit environmental changes.[3]

Organizations have moved into green buildings or refurbished their old office spaces to become greener. The installation of solar panels, the use of glass panels that reflect heat and reduce the need for air conditioning, the greening of the terrace and the construction of vertical gardens are some of the prevalent forms of introducing green in the workplace. Many manufacturing organizations have taken initiatives to green the surrounding landscape by planting trees. PCBL has converted its plant locations into green zones by planting 5,000 plus saplings and has contributed to the cleaning of ponds and rivers near its manufacturing units.

---

[3] https://www.worldgbc.org/what-green-building

Green buildings are a symbol of the organization's commitment to the environment. Retrofitting for green infrastructure and construction of green premises add to the costs, as these technologies require huge capital investments, but they lead to savings in energy and resource utilization in the years to come. Hence, the adoption of green infrastructure is a sensible business choice that will lead to long-term payoffs.

CESC Ltd. has taken initiatives to green its surroundings and it also has a herbal garden in its plant premises with specimens of rare medicinal and exotic plants. These not only add to the aesthetics but are also used for corporate gifting purpose. Research shows that growing trees in and around plants and factories can help in reducing pollution, as trees can absorb 27 per cent of gaseous pollutants, such as sulphur dioxide, nitrogen dioxide and reduce particulate matter from the atmosphere.[4]

GOING PAPERLESS

A lot of organizations in the telecom, electricity, airlines and banking industries have taken initiatives to go paperless not only for internal communication. These companies encourage their customers to accept electronic bills. Mobile companies, cab aggregators, banks and utility companies encourage customers to opt for e-bills, thereby reducing the consumption of paper.

The journey of a hundred miles begins with the first step—some organizations have already made giant strides and some have begun their sustainability journey. It is important for all organizations to encourage sustainability initiatives across their value chain. The introduction of green practices would promote pro-environmental behaviour among employees. In the

---

[4] https://nexusnewsfeed.com/article/climate-ecology/treesaround-factories-could-absorb-27-percent-of-air-pollution/

discussion on green practices, the focus has been on the managerial and behavioural component of green practices. The mechanisms of technical processes and operational details are definitely important, but they are beyond the scope of this book.

Let's Reflect

What new ideas for green practices do you have?

A._____

B._____

C._____

D._____

E._____

REFERENCES

Alfred, A. M., & Adam, R. F. (2009). Green management matters regardless. *Academy of Management Perspectives*, *23*(3), 17–26.

Behrend, T. S., Baker, B. A., & Thompson, L. F. (2009). Effects of pro-environmental recruiting messages: The role of organizational reputation. *Journal of Business and Psychology*, *24*(3), 341–350.

Gultekin, P., Mollaoglu-Korkmaz, S., Riley, D. R., & Leicht, R. M. (2013). Process indicators to track effectiveness of high-performance green building projects. *Journal of Construction Engineering and Management*, *139*(12), A4013005.

Kim, A., Kim, Y., & Han, K. (2019). A cross level investigation on the linkage between job satisfaction and voluntary workplace green behavior. *Journal of Business Ethics*, *159*(4), 1199–1214.

Marcus, A. A., Geffen, D. A., & Sexton, K. (2002). *Reinventing environmental regulation: Lessons from Project XL.* Resources for the Future. https://books.google.co.in/books?hl=en&lr=& id=Zo6zWTku_EYC&oi=fnd&pg=PA1&dq=Marcus,+ Geffen+and+Sexton+3M+environment&ots=coYoQtVGjI &sig=CJqxu2UqYqoP2ASYxjJEc1gECAk#v=onepage &q=Marcus%2C%20Geffen%20and%20Sexton%203 M%20environment&f=false

Nohria, N., Groysberg, B., & Lee, L. E. (2008). Employee motivation: A powerful new model. *Harvard Business Review, 86*(7/8), 78–84.

Sammalisto, K., & Brorson, T. (2008). Training and communication in the implementation of environmental management systems (ISO 14001): A case study at the University of Gävle, Sweden. *Journal of Cleaner Production, 16*(3), 299–309.

SUGGESTED READINGS

https://www.worldgbc.org/what-green-building

http://wiprosustainabilityreport.com/16-17/water_ stewardship

ARE ENVIRONMENTAL PERFORMANCE AND GREEN HRM RELATED?

Harsh Dikshit, HR and sustainability consultant, was on his way to the head office of Trisha Motors, one of the leading automotive companies of India. Trisha was a very well-known brand with operations in India and Europe. The brand was trustworthy and well known and had been around for several decades. Harsh wondered why Trisha Motors had never been in the news for its sustainability drive. Being an auto company it was meant to follow some very stringent norms to control emissions. Automobiles are supposed to be heavy polluters, as the entire life cycle of a car involves the usage and consumption of resources that adversely impact the environment. When a vehicle is being manufactured, it involves the usage of metals, plastic, glass and other chemicals, and upon hitting the road, it guzzles several thousand litres of fuel leading to air pollution, and once a car is junked, a part of the discard is non bio-degradable and toxic. Governments have set stringent conditions on engine emissions that the industry has to conform to. Volkswagen, Harsh reflected, did face a lot of flak for fudging emission data and bringing disrepute to the industry for its negative contribution to the environment.

As sustainability was gaining currency in most industries, the auto sector could not have slackened. They responded by changing to green production by substituting some of the raw material with recyclable material and experimenting with changes in the engine design to cut emissions. Many companies were thinking of introducing electric cars with Tesla and the Indian Mahindra Electric[1] being the front runners in introducing this new technology.

BEGINNING OF THE SUSTAINABILITY JOURNEY FOR TRISHA

In the backdrop of these changes, Trisha Motors seemed to be interested in taking their sustainability efforts forward. Harsh had a brief telephonic conversation with Smita Narang, who had recently been appointed CEO of Trisha Motors. Harsh had known Smita since their MBA days, and they had chosen very different paths in life. Harsh had converted his passion for the environment and the planet into his work by founding a sustainability consulting firm after spending a few years in a corporate job. His company not only specialized in sustainability reporting but also helped clients design and execute environment-related projects. Smita did sound very excited about the new sustainability drive that was about to be launched in Trisha Motors. The company wanted to set ambitious sustainability goals for the next decade. Now the big question was whether the organization would be able to meet those stiff targets.

Smita had invited Harsh to prepare a plan to involve HR in this sustainability drive in a big way. From what Harsh had heard, sustainability initiatives had till then been the responsibility of a separate EM department, which worked very closely

---

[1] https://www.mahindraelectric.com/

with manufacturing to integrate sustainability with production processes. Harsh was now being roped in to strengthen the sustainability orientation of the other departments, especially HR.

With all such thoughts running in his mind, Harsh began pouring over the documents and presentation he had prepared for Trisha. On the basis of his vast experience in sustainability consulting, Harsh had developed a conceptual model that linked HRM with the sustainability drive and showed its impact on the organization's environmental performance.

THE SUSTAINABILITY MEETING

Once inside the boardroom, he could see Trisha's Top Management Team waiting for the meeting to begin. Smita set the ball rolling by first making a short presentation to explain why Trisha Motors needed to make sustainability one of its strategic priorities. She began by explaining how Trisha had been on the growth path for the last two decades and how it could continue to grow. But since taking over the leadership of Trisha she had felt that the organization seriously needed to rethink its performance metrics. There were sweeping changes happening in the world outside and the new agenda was sustainability for the corporate. The sustainability drive across industries was gaining momentum and the automobile industry would have to work towards becoming more sustainable. She then took the group through the environmental initiatives taken by the sustainability and manufacturing departments at Trisha. They had changed the vehicle designs to make them more efficient and experimented with the substitution of different raw materials. As an organization, they were conforming to all the environmental laws applicable to their industry. But that did not seem enough. Smita hoped for some active interventions to boost sustainability at Trisha. With this, she introduced Harsh and beckoned him to begin his presentation.

THE CONSULTANT'S PRESENTATION

Harsh began by saying that sustainability is the future of the world. When a lot of organizations around the world are having ambitions to set up colonies on other planets, promote space tourism and even find other habitable planets, a very sensible idea would be to save planet Earth, which has been the natural abode of the human race since the beginning of time. According to him, the current fascination with space exploration (which had its own importance) could not be at the cost of neglecting the well-being of planet Earth. Saving the planet was a very tall order. Can any one person, a group or a large establishment take responsibility? The answer was an emphatic yes. Harsh's passion could very much be seen in the way he made his opening remarks. It was always a good idea to share the big picture and then get into the nitty-gritties of what needs to be done at the micro level.

HARSH'S SUSTAINABILITY FRAMEWORK

Figure 7.1. Conceptual Framework

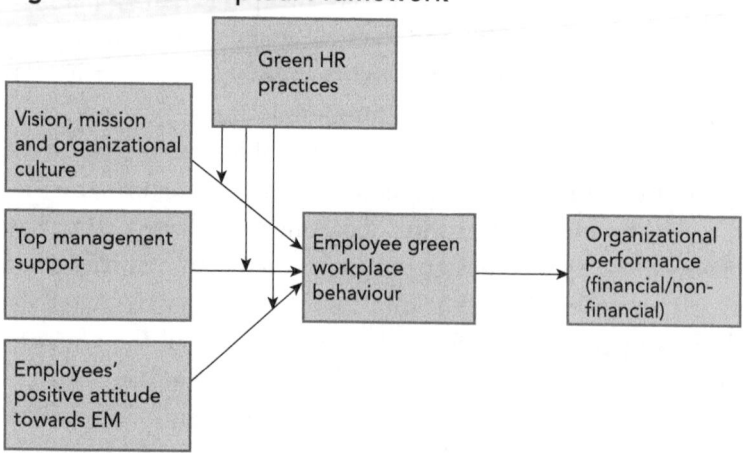

Harsh displayed his model of sustainability and chose to explain the causalities in the reverse order. His first question directed at the senior team was: What would comprise environmental performance? He expectantly looked around hoping to get some responses. VP Marketing said that environmental performance was complex and could not be captured using a single measure. It would comprise financial as well as non-financial parameters.

Harsh nodded in agreement and continued by saying that some of the popular measures could be:

Number of recordable injuries/illnesses	Number/type of reportable releases
Number of lost workday cases	Permitted air emissions
Amount of hazardous waste generated	Amount/type of fuel used
	Amount of water used
Quantity of toxic chemicals released	Total annual EHS operating costs
Number of notices of violation	
Type/volume of non-regulated materials recycled	Number of regulatory inspections
Type/volume of non-regulated materials disposed	Total annual EHS capital costs

Source: Global Environmental Management Initiative (1998).

The aforementioned are some generic measures, and every industry, Harsh continued, can have its own set of measures. For example, in the automobile industry, the popular environmental performance measures could be the following:

Green manufacturing metrics

• Materials used in manufacturing (key materials: paints, steel coils, ferrous castings, non-ferrous castings)

• Electricity consumption per car in one plant (year-wise comparisons can be made to check for trends)

- Usage of water (inclusion of all sources)—year-wise comparison to check for changes (surface water [canal water]), groundwater [tube well water], rainwater, recycled water), water consumption per car in a manufacturing unit in a year

- Source of GHG emission can be fossil fuel combustion for power generation

- Effluents and waste (amount of water discharged from the plant, treatment of effluents, processing and use of recyclable water, production of hazardous wastes—paint sludge, phosphate sludge, ETP sludge, incinerator ash and used oil)

Companies try to reduce the usage of resources and the recycling and repurposing of waste material on a year-on-year basis.[2]

Similarly, the metrics would vary for a steel manufacturing company.

- Environmental impact

- Green cover achievement

- Reduction in CO_2 emission intensity

- Reduction in net water consumption

- Reduction in specific water consumption

- RWH

- Solid waste utilization[3]

---

[2] https://marutistoragenew.blob.core.windows.net/msilintiwebpdf/GREEN_MANUFACTURING.pdf

[3] https://www.tatasteel.com/sustainability/

In spite of being in the services sector, there is scope for an IT company to have sustainability goals. The metrics that could be used are as follows.

1. *Carbon footprint reduction:* Energy efficiency and use of renewable energy

2. *Water management:* Efficient use, recycling and RWH

3. *Waste management:* Reduction, reuse and recycling

4. Supply chain sustainability

Energy efficiency can be increased by functioning in a green building (new infrastructure/retrofitting for conversion to green for the existing building), running energy management programmes, switching to the use of renewable sources of energy and managing a green IT infrastructure to optimize the use of power. Business travel to clients' site and employees' commute to offices daily can be another source of value chain emissions, and this can be cut by reliance on video conferencing, remote teamwork and lesser number of employees physically present at the workplace.[4]

Similarly, for a telecom company such as Airtel, the metrics could be the following:

Green initiatives

• Reduction in CO_2 emissions across network infrastructure

• Reduction in CO_2 emissions per square feet in the facility and reduction in CO_2 emissions per rack in data centre operations

---

[4] https://www.tcs.com/content/dam/tcs/pdf/discover-tcs/investor-relations/corporate-sustainability/GRI-Sustainability-Report-2018-2019.pdf

- Savings of millions of sheets of paper on paperless billing initiatives

- Paperless verification process based on the Aadhaar card

- Recycling of e-waste and refurbishing of the DTH set top boxes[5]

UNDERSTANDING THE LINKAGES

Harsh continued with the presentation by now shifting the focus to how environmental performance can be achieved by initiating several changes in processes, technologies, work redesigning and active engagement with waste production. The focus needs to be on reducing the consumption of resources in the production of goods and services, and also if waste generation cannot be reduced, initiatives can be taken to recycle, reuse and repurpose waste products.

Harsh sensed that the group was listening intently and seemed to be interested. Harsh continued by saying, 'When we talk about results, we also need to look at the factors that are responsible for giving us those outcomes. We need to understand that having a separate department entrusted with environmental responsibilities may not suffice.' For organizations that make EM their priority, the involvement of all employees is a must. This has also been true for the quality movement. When organizations adopted the total quality management philosophy, it was imperative to teach all employees the methods required for maintaining quality and have employee participation in the form of quality circles to facilitate the generation of good quality management ideas.

---

[5] https://www.airtel.in/press-release/07-2017/airtel-releases-2017-india-sustainability-report

EMPLOYEE PRO-ENVIRONMENTAL BEHAVIOUR CAN MAKE A BIG DIFFERENCE

Organizations that are sustainability leaders try to develop a green orientation in all their employees so that their actions would be imbued with environmental consideration. All the metrics that have been discussed earlier in this presentation are not based on any one-time action of organizations. Rather they are the accumulation of a number of incremental ideas that helped optimize resource utilization. When employees demonstrate pro-environmental behaviour, they think about the environmental consequences of every action. For most employees, it may mean thinking twice before taking a printout or planning a business trip or switching off the lights before leaving the office. Actions could be as mundane as these or may include consideration of the environmental consequences of a new product design or a new production process. Very often, some minor changes can lead to great energy savings. Harsh wondered, by giving a fictional example. In the movie *Mission Mangal*, the idea for saving costs for the Mars Mission came from a scientist who saved cooking gas by frying puris in hot oil that did not need further heating. It was a simple and highly effective idea that was used to design the satellite for the Mars expedition at very nominal project expenditure. The story may seem ludicrous and may not appeal to scientific sensibilities, but the message is worth emulating. A good idea can come from any employee, not necessarily the top brass of any organization. So encouraging all employees across all levels to believe in sustainability and persistently work towards it would give a critical mass to the sustainability drive in organizations.

GREEN HRM

Next, we need to look at why would employees be interested in demonstrating environmentally sensitive behaviour?

Their green behaviour would be influenced by a number of factors. One of the significant factors would be GHRM. If all HR processes are sustainability oriented, it will make it easier for organizations to encourage employees to think and act upon environmental matters. If an organization includes environment-related KPIs in employee PM, employees will start taking their environmental responsibilities seriously. If energy utilization, water consumption and waste generation can be measured department wise, the persons in charge of those departments can be made accountable for the same. When employees are given rewards and recognition for their contribution to the environment, it would go a long way in strengthening their commitment to the environment. Similarly, when employees are given environmental training, it helps to make them environmentally conscious and show the commitment of the organizations to the environment. Training could be given in new processes that help to optimize resource usage. Selecting employees on the basis of their passion for the environment would also go a long way in making the organization sustainable. If individuals with pro-green attitudes join the organization, it would be much easier to involve them in environmental initiatives rather than converting people who have no interest in the environment. Inducting people with green values would negate any resistance in practising green behaviour, to become green champions.

Do you know about Unilever's sustainable living plan?

Read more at https://www.unilever.com/sustainable-living/

TOP MANAGEMENT SUPPORT

Again, GHRM cannot work in isolation if the top management does not support green in the organization. We need leaders to be committed to sustainability and help the organization see the need for it. The top leadership team needs to provide the vision for a sustainable future and resources to make the organization sustainable. Unilever has embarked upon the sustainability journey by kick-starting the 'Sustainable Living Plan' in 2010. The motivation came from the then CEO, Mr Paul Polman, who said:

> I don't think our fiduciary duty is to put shareholders first. I say the opposite. What we firmly believe is that if we focus our company on improving the lives of the world's citizens and come up with genuine sustainable solutions, we are more in synch with consumers and society and ultimately this will result in good shareholder returns.

The company stated that its long-term mission of doubling its revenues and reducing the environmental impact by half was supposed to be applicable to all of Unilever's product lines and value chains. The plan focused on sustainable sourcing, greening agro-supply chains and changing consumer's end behaviour to reduce energy costs by cutting the usage of hot water in showers and washing of clothes. Paul Polman is well known for his sustainable leadership through which he upholds the environmental needs of the company's operations and and champions social causes. Thus, a leader who believes in sustainability, along with the support of the senior team, becomes an important catalyst in bringing about the social change. Harsh digressed from his narration to comment that now it was the responsibility of Trisha Motors' top team to believe in the environmental agenda and put all its support behind the sustainability plans to make them work.

Top leadership not only redefines the new mission and vision that will have sustainability as an important theme, but their message and persistence positively shape the values and beliefs the organization is going to uphold. The Chevron mission statement reads as follows: 'Our Company's foundation is built on our values, which distinguish us and guide our actions. We conduct our business in a socially responsible and ethical manner. We respect the law, support universal human rights, protect the environment and benefit the communities where we work' and Adidas' mission statement goes as follows: 'We are a global organisation that is socially and environmentally responsible, that embraces creativity and diversity and is financially rewarding for our employees and shareholders.' The leader also needs to communicate sustainability messages to motivate people to start practising it.

Sustainability needs to be consolidated with the strategy of the organization. This would mean integrating the sustainability component into the production strategy, the HRM strategy and the marketing strategy to ensure that all departments work in tandem to meet the green targets. The top leadership has to convey this message to the front lines so that all employees can buy into this message.

Besides strategy and communication, the top leadership needs to support such efforts with resources—monetary and otherwise. If the building is to be retrofitted to become green, it will involve costs, if the employees have to be given environmental training, there is money to be spent. Similarly, when sustainability-based KPIs and KRAs become part of the managers' responsibility, they have to devote time and effort to work on sustainability projects. Top management has to encourage employees to devote their time to work on sustainability projects. This is the human resource investment in sustainability that needs to be backed up by the top brass.

ORGANIZATIONAL CULTURE CAN SHAPE BEHAVIOUR

All the leadership and HRM efforts would lead to changes in the organizational culture. Culture will become sustainable when people will begin to understand the importance and role of sustainability and green practices in the organization and practise green behaviour. Cultural change will happen when the leader demonstrates green behaviour by being the role model.

This whole process of green leadership and sustainability would be greatly facilitated when employees already believe in sustainability as individuals. There has to be a favourable attitude towards the environment and this would facilitate the transition of the organization to becoming sustainable one. So at Trisha Motors, too, you need to identify people who value the environment, and train and motivate them to bring about change in people and processes to make the organization green.

WHAT NEXT?

The explanation had been a long one in which Harsh tried to tie together all the components of the model to explain their impact on organizational environmental performance. Harsh wondered, and he looked around to sense the group's reactions. They seemed to agree with him. Some were nodding and discussing among themselves how Trisha could use the model. So far, Harsh had not faced any resistance and grilling from the top management team. This seemed to be a good sign. Once the top management supported sustainability, it would be easier to work through the hierarchy at Trisha. Smita also seemed happy with Harsh's presentation. This left Harsh wondering about the next question: When was the team meeting again to define actionable targets?

Lessons to learn

1. Top management needs to truly demonstrate its commitment to sustainability.

2. Support would mean investing in sustainability infrastructure and integrating sustainability with the strategy.

3. Redefining the vision and mission statement to make it environment inclusive, spelling out how the organization would demonstrate its environmental responsibility.

4. Integrating sustainability with the strategy of HRM, marketing, production and supply chains. Focusing on anyone will not give great results.

5. Encouraging employees to demonstrate pro-environmental behaviour by making all HR processes green.

6. Mapping the environmental performance of the organization by identifying tangible measures and capturing data to understand change in them on a year-on-year basis.

7. Connecting the measures identified with the actions and behaviours demonstrated by employees so that their behaviour can be improved for better results.

REFERENCES

Global Environmental Management Initiative. (1998). Measuring environmental performance: A primer and survey of metrics in use. https://www.greenbiz.com/sites/default/files/document/CustomO16C45F61031.pdf

Schaefer, A., & Harvey, B. (1998). Stage models of corporate 'greening': A critical evaluation. *Business Strategy and the Environment*, 7(3), 109–123.

SUGGESTED READINGS

https://www.nationalgeographic.com/environment/green-guide/buying-guides/car/environmental-impact/

https://www.theguardian.com/sustainable-business/paul-polman-unilever-sustainable-living-plan

https://www.europeanceo.com/business-and-management/unilever-ceo-paul-polman-is-redefining-sustainable-business/

https://www.europeanceo.com/business-and-management/unilever-ceo-paul-polman-is-redefining-sustainable-business/

https://www.linkedin.com/pulse/20140624160539-41033175-7-mission-statements-that-inspire-sustainability/

TRIPLE BOTTOM LINE: LEVERAGING GREEN HR PRACTICES

It is true that the primary objective of an organization is to maximize its financial performance. However, considering only financial performance cannot be the primary motive of an organization. With the heightening of stakeholders' awareness and expectations, there has been a need to employ holistic measures for understanding what can be defined as performance. The argument here is that only financial performance cannot be the indicator of a firm's success. Rather, understanding the welfare of employees who are the source of the competitive advantage of the firm, as well as managing resources in such a manner that environmental harm is minimal along with earning profitability, must be the key to success.

Thus, here comes the concept of TBL, which means that the performance of a company is the enactment of the PPP.

The triple P or TBL framework was introduced initially in 1997 by Elkington. In Elkington's words, 'the TBL agenda focuses corporations not just on the economic value that they add, but also on the environmental and social value that they add—or destroy.'

As per Elkington, there was a need to coin terms that would have familiarity with business language. When the initial idea of triple P took shape, the author was surprised at its simplicity and was totally certain that it was already in practice, synergy and connection with dots was missing. Moreover, contemporary research confirmed that triple P was not part of the mainstream. Thus, instead of taking ownership for the concept by using protective mechanisms, one can try to make it popular by assembling the new concept through journal articles and consulting reports. Later the book written by him, *Cannibals with Forks: The Triple Bottom Line of 21st Century Business*, became very popular. Moreover, the concept of TBL has received official endorsement as a framework for sustainability.

Comprehensively, the term has captured the whole set of values, issues and processes that companies must address in order to reduce harm resulting from their business activities. The TBL or 'the three pillars' capture a large scale of values and criteria for calculating organizational as well as societal success, not only from economic viewpoints but also from ecological and social outlooks. In pragmatic terms, TBL accounting means expanding the traditional reporting framework for considering ecological and social performance in addition to financial performance.

It implicates being well aware of company's mission and deliberately taking into account all the needs of stakeholders such as shareholders, customers, employees, business partners, governments, local communities and the public.[1]

Although earlier organizations were taking initiatives in each of these areas and were reporting under those heads, the three dimensions were treated in isolation with varying degrees of impact. The popularized concept, triple P, has tagged all three

---

[1] https://www.ifc.org/wps/wcm/connect/topics_ext_content/ifc_external_corporate_site/sustainability-atifc/publications/publications_report_sustainability2003__wci__1319578390109

parameters together to construct a comprehensive and mutually reinforcing framework to provide aid in strategic and corporate performance measurement.

In the Indian perspective, for example, the BRR has become a mandatory requirement after the Companies Act, 2013. SEBI after issuing a vide circular mandated that BRR shall be a part of the annual report. SEBI has recommended that 'integrated reporting may be adopted on a voluntary basis from the fiscal year 2017–18 by (the) top 500 companies which are required to prepare BRR.' And the corporate world has taken the environment and sustainability goals positively and, in the following year, around 30 firms in India published their integrated reports.

In addition, there are a number of voluntary and non-voluntary reporting initiatives that companies undertake to reach out to their global stakeholders. These include GRI standards, UN global compact guidelines, UNFCC, UN's SDGs, etc. Of the world's largest 250 corporations, 35 different countries participate in GRI reporting. Ninety-two per cent of companies report their sustainability performance, and 74 per cent use GRI standards to do so. In the GRI databases, currently 35,518 reports are available. Organizations across the world report on how they reduce their environmental footprints, engage with stakeholders, adopt fair social practices or embed sustainability into their daily business, research and development as well as marketing practices.

In 2014, India took the initiative of becoming one of the first countries to enforce the legal requirement that large and medium-sized companies devote 2 per cent of their profits to social development projects. Tata Steel Ltd was one of the early adopters of sustainability reporting in India. It had come up with its first integrated report in 2015–2016. However, from 2001, Tata Motors started reporting their sustainability performance on the basis of GRI guidelines.

Associated Cement Companies (ACC) Limited, India's leading cement and concrete manufacturer, is one of India's other leading adopters of GRI Standards. Mr K. N. Rao, Director Energy and Environment at ACC, stated about the value of GRI reporting, 'It's a moment of pride for ACC Limited to become the first company in India to release its externally assured sustainable development report 2016 as per new GRI standards.'

Mr Naresh Patil, Deputy Chief Sustainability Officer at Mahindra Group, mentioned:

> Sustainability reporting helps in monitoring and improving a company's environmental, social and economic performance. This non-financial report is also of interest to stakeholders, particularly investors, for evaluating the environmental, social and ethical risks which can impact company's profits. The GRI Standards will be of immense help especially in light of SEBI's recent announcement on 'Integrated Reporting'. Mahindra & Mahindra Limited will be publishing its first integrated report this year and we look forward to taking our integrated reporting further using the GRI Standards.

But, unfortunately, out of 8,691 reports of GRI in 2018, only a handful of 122 reports are published by Indian companies. These handful companies that participate in GRI reporting can truly be called companies with an integrated approach in terms of sustainability.

On the other hand, few companies having started providing information related to some of the areas but that is very scattered, thus does not seem fulfilling the purpose of GRI. This is because most companies do not realize the significant difference between installing solar panels and planting trees to show a reduction in carbon footprint and proactively recognize and seek business opportunities in a low-carbon world.

Disclosure on action on climate change is a top reporting subject in China and, across countries, part of the Organisation for Economic Co-operation and Development (OECD). The OECD came into existence in 1961, and 37 countries were its founding members. The forum was dedicated and committed to providing a platform for seeking solutions to common issues and problems that occur while working in the global scenario. It was committed for maintaining democracy in the international market economy while identifying best practices. In India, priority is given to economic development with effective corporate reporting of climate change data with holistic efforts to reach the second-degree level, as set out in the Paris Agreement.

Thus, there are ways for assessing the performance in line with TBL. To start with

> the Environmental Impact Assessment (EIA) process tries to assess and estimate the total impact on environment of certain policies, programs, practices and further actions of the organization. This is a systematic process and the total audit needs to be presented to the decision makers as suggested in the guidelines. (Schaefer & Harvey, 1998)

On the other hand, in the social impact assessment (SIA), the 'organization's process of assessing the activities, policies and practices are evaluated to see the impact on society as a whole and to also predict whether there will be some social consequences on the society' (Vanclay, 2004, pp. 27–39).

In addition to the EIA and SIA, organizations need to prepare the EP report as well. EP is actually the company's annual financial performance report which covers various parameters that can be used to assess the company's financial health. These parameters include the ratio of market capitalization to book value investments in human capital, research and development, payment of salaries, incentives, bonuses, benefits, community development initiatives and the value and location of out-sourced goods and services (Elkington, 2013).

TBL has gained significant popularity in general in the last two decades as it serves as a handy tool to measure holistic performance and provides an opportunity to strengthen each of the parameters.

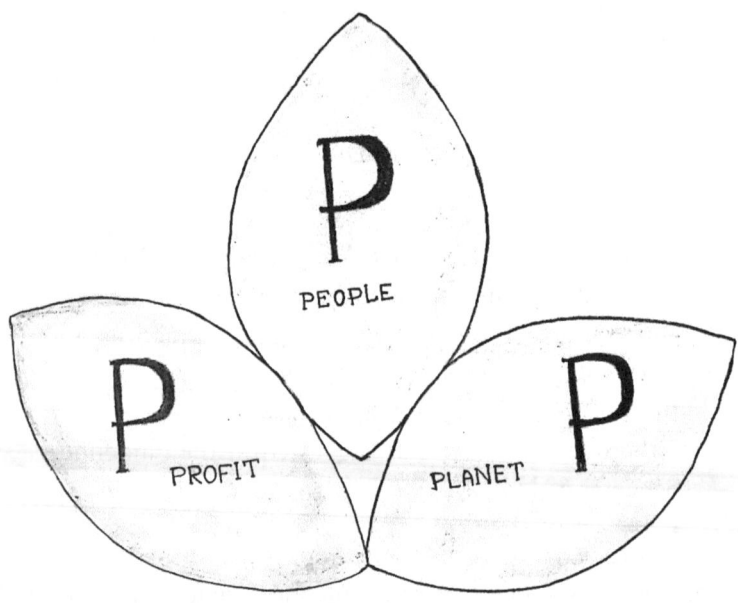

THREE DIMENSIONS OF TRIPLE P

Profits or the economic dimension: It measures the economic value of the organization, which would serve to support the existence and long-run economic viability. Quantifiable measures include spending in R&D, human capital investments, value of market capitalization, remuneration, etc.

People or the social value: This dimension endorses the need to institutionalize good human resource practices and to provide support to the community. The primary focus is to carry out human resource practices inside and outside the boundary of the organization that not only cares for basic requirements of the people but also supports their personal and professional requirements, handholding and overall development. Important metrics that could be included are employee relations, health and safety, ratio of wages to cost of living, non-discrimination, indigenous rights, the impact of community involvement and customer satisfaction.

Planet or the environmental value: This parameter focuses on reducing the harmful environmental impact of the organization. It includes optimization in the consumption of resources, increase in the usage of sustainable assets and a check on the ecological footprint of the organization. Social performance addresses the interactions between an organization and its community. Environmental performance includes a number of factors, such as the amount of energy consumed and its origin, resource and material usage, emissions, effluents and waste management, land use and management of habitats. Social performance addresses interactions between an organization and its community, including issues such as employee relations, health and safety, ratio of wages to cost of living, non-discrimination, indigenous rights, impact of community involvement and customer satisfaction.

A closer look at each dimension reveals that, though all three aspects are interdependent, they are mutually reinforcing. The 'TBL' is mostly described as follows:

- Social performance, environmental performance and EP
- SD, sustainable environment and sustainable communities

- Impact on society, the environment and economic sustainability
- Economic, environmental and social sustainability
- Economic prosperity, environmental quality and social justice
- Economic growth, ecological balance and social progress
- Economic growth, social progress and environmental health
- Economy, environment and equity
- PPP

TRIPLE BOTTOM LINE/SUSTAINABILITY REPORTING

TBL reporting is the practice of measurement as well as disclosure and being accountable to internal and external stakeholders for organizational performance towards the attainment of the goal of SD. Sustainability reporting is a broad term used to describe the reporting on economic, environmental and social impacts. Here, the example of the energy company CESC in brief is given for reference.

Calcutta Electric Supply Corporation

Water management
1. Low-flow water faucets in all toilets
2. Installation of water management system for cooling tower

Energy management
1. Energy-efficient chillers and cooling towers
2. Energy-efficient chiller pump plants

---

3. Compact fluorescent lamps (CFLs) replaced by energy-efficient LED lights

4. Replacement of old tube lights with energy-efficient T5 tube lights

5. Occupancy and lux-level sensors for the judicial usage of energy

Resource management

1. Sun-reflective paint on rooftop

2. Maximum usage of natural daylight

3. Building temperature moderation

4. Waste reduction

5. Improved indoor air quality

6. Improved health and productivity of occupants

7. Ten per cent additional FAR

Planet

Water consumption reduced by 3 lakh litres per year

Energy consumption reduced by more than 22 per cent from 2012 levels

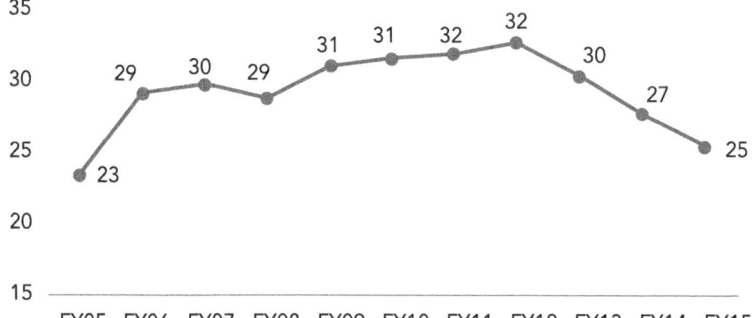

Some of the major steps that have been taken to reduce energy consumption were the replacement of 500 CFLs in common areas of the entire CESC House with highly energy-efficient LED lighting, which led to annual electricity savings of 79,935 units and a carbon footprint reduction of 120 tonnes of CO_2. They have also planted 4,490 equivalent number of trees.

In one of Elkington's recent works, the author shares insights into the development of this concept. As he recounts, there was no 'eureka' moment in which this concept flashed through his mind. He was rather searching for a new vocabulary to express and broaden the environmental objectives.

Elkington has introduced a very interesting typology of organizations in terms of its responsiveness to environmental concerns. The organizational model developed by Elkington (2013) and the revolutions are discussed further.

	Low Impact	High Impact
Regenerative (increasing returns)	Butterflies	Honeybees
	Corporate butterflies work towards sustainability and their efforts are showcased in the public domain.	A sustainable business model, albeit based on constant innovation;
	• A sustainable business model, though it may become less sustainable as success drives growth, expansion and increasing reliance on financial markets and large corporate partners;	• A clear and appropriate set of ethics-based business principles; • Strategic sustainable management of natural resources;
	• A strong commitment to the CSR and SD agenda;	• A capacity for sustained heavy lifting;

	Low Impact	High Impact
	• The tendency to define its position by referring to locusts and caterpillars; • A wide network, though not among locusts or honeybees; • increased involvement in symbiotic relationships; • persistent indirect links to degenerative activities; • a potential capacity to trigger quite disproportionate changes in consumer priorities and, as a result, in the wider economic system • High visibility and a disproportionately powerful voice for such economic lightweights	• The sociability and evolution of powerful symbiotic partnerships; • Sustainable production of natural, human, social, institutional and cultural capital • A capacity to moderate the impacts of corporate caterpillars in its supply chain, to learn from the mistakes of corporate locusts and, in certain circumstances, to boost the efforts of corporate butterflies.
Degenerative (decreasing returns)	Caterpillars Caterpillars are offenders too, but their environmental destruction is within a limited zone. • Generate relatively local impacts, most of the time; • Show a single-minded dedication to the business task at hand; • Depend on a high 'burn rate', though usually on forms of capital that are renewable over time;	Locusts Destruction of natural, human, social and economic capital; • Collectively, an unsustainable 'burn rate', potentially creating regional or even global impacts; • A business model that is unsustainable over the long run; • Periods of invisibility, when it is hard to discern the impending threat;

(Continued)

	Low Impact	High Impact
	• Operate on a business model that is unsustainable when projected forward into a more equitable world of 8 to 10 billion people; • Have the potential for transformation into a more sustainable guise, often based on a mutated business model • Operate in sectors where there is evidence that pioneering companies are already starting to metamorphose towards more sustainable forms of value creation	• A tendency to swarm (think of gold rushes), overwhelming the carrying capacity of social systems, ecosystems or economies • An incapacity to foresee negative system effects, coupled with an unwillingness to heed early warnings and learn from mistakes

Source: Elkington (2013).

ENHANCING TBL REPORTING IN INDIA

Although there is so much growth in the popularity of the concept, the analysis reveals that, till date, the adoption of corporate sustainability reporting in India is not uniform. In spite of the merits of this mode of organizational assessment, this has not found absolute acceptance. As per India Inc., at present, there are a significant number of companies, especially smaller entities, that do not report on their social or environmental performance. The majority of organizations still perpetuate the traditional financial reporting system only as the measure of the organization's performance. The concern and slow growth in sustainability reporting can be attributed to two factors.

First, sustainability reporting is still in its dawning phase. Proponents and practitioners are struggling with the questions of best practice and the requisite character of future reporting and principles. There is less standardization in terms of measures, codes or guiding principles.

Second, financial reporting, which has a clear measurement of sustainability issues, tends to be more qualitative in nature and addresses broader groups of stakeholders. Such ambiguity and diversity contribute to the hindrance of establishment of best reporting practices, codes, principles and guidelines.

Until these issues are reasonably addressed, TBL reporting cannot be not expected to experience widespread adoption.

TBL IN PRACTICES

There are Indian companies reporting sustainability from the hospitality, manufacturing, banking, telecom and other sectors. There are not many prominent Indian organizations that are part of this sustainability initiative. A few out of them, which are taking initiatives in this direction, are documented. In this list, Maruti Suzuki comes first and the practices are explained in great detail covering all three aspects, that is, PPP. Other than that, PCBL, Larsen & Toubro (L&T), ITC and Marriott International are few more on this list. These companies are pioneers in the TBL approach and have taken a number of steps in this direction. Detailed documentation is given further.

Maruti Suzuki Motor Corporation

Maruti Suzuki Motor Corporation is an environment-friendly company. The company is certified with ISO 14001 standard and believes in sustainability-related practices in the supply chain through guidelines, handholding and capacity building. It believes in the philosophy of 'smaller, fewer, lighter, shorter and neater'. The company is endeavoured to ensuring the optimum utilization of raw materials and to minimizing waste throughout the life cycle of the vehicle.

EIA is done by Maruti Suzuki to manage environment-related actions by the company.

The commitment of the company is based on certain fundamentally accepted principles aimed at reducing pressure on the environment.

With collaborative efforts with all stakeholders, that is, clients, vendors, suppliers, nearby communities, the company is successful in implementing EMS with the facilities of its suppliers.

By the FY2017, 86 per cent of its Tier 1 suppliers had implemented EMS in their facilities. More than that 100 per cent of its suppliers had already signed the 'Green Procurement Guidelines' (GPGs). The GPGs are based on the EU's end-of-life vehicle standards for auto parts. These guidelines are referred to for the recycling of auto parts in an eco-friendly manner at the end of their life cycle.

PLANET: REDUCING NATURAL RESOURCES, WATER AND ENERGY

One of the initiatives as taken by the company to reduce the consumption of water was to initiate the facility of 'dry wash' for cars at its workshops. The special 'biodegradable dry chemical' facility not only helps in reducing the usage of water but is also a much speedier process. The use of the new automated car and underbody washing system saves up to 20 per cent of total water consumption, claims Maruti Suzuki. As of 30 March 2017, 880 workshops were equipped with this system.

In FY 2016–2017, 200 litres of water was saved per manufactured vehicle, while water demand for manufacturing units was reduced by 81,032 cu. m.

Overall freshwater consumption reduced by 5 per cent and the water intensity (water consumption per vehicle manufactured) decreased to 1.38 cu. m in FY2018 from 1.48 cu. m in the previous year.

As a result, the requirement of fresh water had gone down. The amount of water that is saved by the company per annum is 216 million litres because of this. The result is that only '5 per cent of freshwater demand of manufacturing is met by ground water'.

Another step in this direction is recycling the entire volume of industrial and domestic effluents through ETPs and STPs. The company recycled and reused water at its facilities, claiming that 60 per cent of water demand is met through recycled water. Thus, recycled water is used in the manufacturing and horticulture process, which is 73 per cent and 27 per cent, respectively.

Special emphasis is given to source from local suppliers. This not only helps in saving time of logistics transportation but also in giving opportunity to local economic growth.

At Maruti, natural gases are used for meeting the requirements of energy, which is almost 95 per cent, and the remaining 5 per cent is met from other sources, such as diesel and grid electricity, and a small portion from solar.

In FY 2017–2018, iMaruti claimed that it had saved 830,367 tonnes of CO_2 since 2006, while 0.12 J of energy was saved per vehicle manufactured due to clean and fuel-efficient technologies (base year 2005–2006). The company primarily deployed alternative fuels such as LPG, CNG and smart hybrid vehicle from Suzuki (SHVS) vehicles.

The R&D efforts have resulted in fuel-efficient engine technologies such as the i-GPI CNG engine and smart hybrid vehicle from Suzuki (SHVS).

In Maruti, the energy consumption per vehicle manufactured had been gone down (0.03 GJ over two FYs 2016–2017 and 2017–2018).

In FY2018, the total GHG emissions of the company (both Scope 1 and Scope 2) increased over the last reporting period, while the GHG emission intensity (Scope 1 and Scope 2 total emissions per vehicle manufactured) reduced marginally (0.263 to 0.261 GJ).

The automated oil management system not only protects against oil spillage but also offers greater control and a method to monitor the quantity of oil used, thereby preventing wastage and improving productivity.

On waste management, hazardous waste was sent to the cement industry for further co-processing and the remaining to the authority recyclers.

PEOPLE

Some of the community-related works include the development and adoption of villages, safety of roads and skill development. These projects are also taken as seriously as any other business activity.

Skill development aspect includes the adoption of industrial training institutes (ITIs) for improving skills among youth in the automobile industry. For this, a number of partnerships are made with state governments. They set up 'automobile skill enhancement centres' in some of the ITIs. These centres are utilized for providing training to youth by full-time trainers supported by the company.

In this direction, another initiative 'Japan-India Institute for Manufacturing' at A. S. Patel (Pvt) ITI in Ganpat University,

Mehsana, Gujarat, was set up in FY2016–2017. Under this, the governments of Japan and India signed an agreement to create a pool of skilled manpower for manufacturing in India. As part of this, Maruti established the first one. Practical shop-floor trainings were organized such as Kaizen and quality circles for youth.

Another initiative in this direction includes adoption of 26 villages around its factories in Haryana (Gurugram, Manesar and Rohtak) and Gujarat (Hansalpur). These villages were supported for improving their infrastructure such as repairing work of streets, construction of community halls and improvement in the areas of water and sanitation. Other than that, expert agencies were deployed to better assess the specific village-level needs.

For upgrading the infrastructure of government schools, separate toilet blocks for both boys and girls were constructed. Other than that, water tanks, furniture, lights and fans were installed, and blackboards were repaired since 2006–2007. Under this, till 2017, 47 schools were supported and 25,000 students benefitted under this. Towards improving learning and training teachers, audiovisual devices were installed. Additional teachers were recruited and trained. Meritorious students were offered scholarships. Students got inputs on how to maintain their basic hygiene, which helped them maintain both their physical and mental health.

PROFIT

In FY2018, the expenditure of the company in the CSR fund was ₹125.08 crore.

The company had spent ₹18.74 million as a capital investment for energy conservation equipment in FY2017–2018.

The company spent ₹1,250.8 million in FY2017–2018 on special projects related to sustainability.

The highest amount of money was spent on projects related to water and sanitation, road safety and upgradation of government training institutes.

Source: Annual report and sustainability reporting of Maruti Suzuki.[2]

Phillips Carbon Black Ltd

PCBL has adopted the TBL framework to evaluate their performance in a broader perspective to create greater business value. The TBL is a framework or theory that recommends companies commit to focus on social and environmental concerns just as they do on profits.

It is sensitive to the needs and expectations of the community. PCBL is far ahead in preserving and enriching the environment as far as possible. Policies and projects are implemented in a number of areas related to education, the environment and sustainability, health and community development, as well as to take care of, and support and facilitate the development of the underprivileged sections of society and to give them the needed support and development opportunities.

PLANET

Some of the initiatives taken by PCBL include the cleaning of ponds and rivers near its manufacturing units. For creating green belts inside and outside its factory premises, plantation of saplings is a continuous drive. The company believes in the production and use of organic products, including fertilizers,

---

[2] https://marutistoragenew.blob.core.windows.net/msilintiwebpdf/Integrated_Report_2018_19_Low.pdf

cow fodder and grass, to the drought-prone villages located in the close vicinity to its plants.

PEOPLE

The five pillars towards people philosophy of the company are 'people philosophy–leadership, culture, capabilities, demography and rewards'. People philosophy–leadership pillar is based on the B2MOM (big idea, business theme, methods, obstacle and measures) concept. The concept gives a lot of emphasis on the PM system. The B2MOM focuses on team performance while empowering employees. Moreover, leadership skills are identified and potential support is provided to further promote employees that have requisite trains. Moreover, the culture in the organization is quiet transparent and engrosses its core values. The communication platform 'Sampark Live' (a real-time video-based platform) plays an important role in this direction.

The 'capability-building initiatives' as a philosophy were introduced in 2018. These capability-building initiatives include 'Virtual Gurukul (an online training platform), Embark PCBLite (an e-induction module for newly joined employees), and Pragati (a workshop to align the mind-set of the employees across the organization hierarchy towards the Company's business)'.

Various programmes that support and develop the infrastructure at schools are employed by PCBL. Some of the programmes include 'computer literacy programs, facilitation of tuitions, distribution of school-aid materials, donation towards food distribution, cultural activities at schools for underprivileged students and distribution of uniforms to the community children'.

Under the Government of India, 'Swachh Bharat Abhiyan', the company has constructed individual household toilets.

In addition, for benefiting the local community, medical aids (including diagnosis and consultation) are given. It had organized a 'pulse polio immunization camp' for children of nearby villages. Fodder for cattle, donation of funds under the Chief Minister Relief Fund, financial assistance for social projects in backward areas, improvement of basic infrastructure, like roads in the villages adjoining our factories, are some more contributions.

For maintaining safety, employees are empowered and encouraged by taking the ownership to get indulged in safe processes. For understanding and promoting 'customized risk-based' training programmes, workshops are organized across manufacturing units and plants for achieving 'zero fatal accidents' at plants.

Source: Annual report and sustainability reporting of PCBL.[3]

Larsen & Toubro

The L&T group has established sustainability under the three parameters of TBL. Some of them are the usage of natural materials in the construction and manufacturing facilities. A lot of emphasis is given for identifying the best alternative or substitute that can either be replaced with natural materials or can at least be recycled.

PLANET

Two campuses of L&T which are located in Powai (Mumbai) and Chennai are actually power neutral. The continuous efforts of the company to reduce carbon emission intensity

---

[3] https://www.pcblltd.com/annual-reports/

at campuses and project sites brought positive results and gave a positive push to the company in the direction to be even more resilient towards improved outcomes. L&T is water positive at all 24 campuses. L&T campuses have more than 35 per cent open area available under green cover.

- More than 150,000 trees are nurtured in the L&T campuses.
- In 2016–2017, L&T planted more than 295,000 trees at campuses and project sites.
- The company monitors tree plantation through a tree inventory portal.
- Guests are felicitated either by planting a sapling or by presenting a Tree Certificate at key campuses.
- Tree plantation and maintenance is part of integrated community development.

The overall plan of the CSR project was adopted across villages in Rajasthan, Maharashtra and Tamil Nadu.

PEOPLE

L&T has initiated a number of programmes for the welfare of people. Safety and related efforts are given the utmost importance. The group has institutionalized safety precepts and practices into their way of working at projects, plants and offices. Zero harm is the motive, and culture has already gained ground. Actions are seen on the ground and are very effective. Not only has it mitigated risk through sound management encompassing the entire cycle, from identification of risk to review of controls, but it also has become a vital component of sustainability.

At L&T, specialist risk managers are trained and equipped to study likely eventualities and to ensure that steps are taken to mitigate negative outcomes.

This has led to continual improvement in safety performance at the workplace. It continues to work in six thrust areas identified as a part of their 'Zero Accident Vision 2021'.

As it is in the day-to-day culture of the organization, many in-house functional and technical capacity-building programmes on sustainability and climate change are conducted that include the following:

- Confederation of Indian Industry–Green Business Centre certified programme on energy efficiency and climate change
- Certified Sustainability Assurance Practitioner programmes
- Preparatory programmes for the energy auditor and energy manager examination conducted by the Bureau of Energy Efficiency
- Training programme on the GreenCo Rating System for companies
- GRI standards reporting framework
- Prayag (the induction programme for new employees) which covers SD and climate change topics along with EHS and human rights

Profit: Green Portfolio Management

L&T's portfolio of green products and services contributed to 28.99 per cent of overall sales, which is an increase of 22.7 per cent over the previous year.

There was an increase in direct GHG emission intensity by 14.3 per cent per turnover in 2016–2017. This has become possible as the company used energy-intensive project execution stages and variable project cycles across businesses.

In 2016–2017, an increase of 9.4 per cent in energy conservation was achieved.

A total of 22 L&T campuses, 17 domestic marketing network offices and L&T House and Leadership Development Academy, Lonavala, had zero reported accidents in 2016–2017.

It achieved 11 per cent reduction in water consumption intensity (KL/workforce) in 2016–2017.

All 24 L&T campuses in India are now 'water positive'.

RWH increased by 5 per cent.

There has been an increase in domestic wastewater recycling from 48 per cent to 57 per cent.

It reached out to 1.47 million beneficiaries in 2016–2017 under CSR.

In 2016–2017, zinc recycling increased by 2.1 per cent and crushed sand recycling increased by 33 per cent.

It is the endeavour of L&T to increase the recycling of steel and fly ash.

Source: Annual report and sustainability reporting of L&T.[4]

Mahindra & Mahindra

PLANET

Mahindra Research Valley inaugurated its on-site 420 KW solar power plant to cater to a portion of its power requirement through green energy, which is spread over an area of 4,200 sq. m.

---

[4] https://corpwebstorage.blob.core.windows.net/media/41101/lt-integrated-report-2018-19-dt20191015.pdf

M&M initiated its plantation movement 'Hariyali' in FY2017–2018. Under this, approximately 1.5 million trees were planted. On top of that, 1,302,488 trees were planted alone by M&M; 15.38 million saplings were implanted under Project Hariyali.

The water consumption level for the plant in FY2016–2017 stood at 46,613 cu. m from the external source, whereas the water saving was 351,693 cu.m^3.

RWH of 3.8 lakh m was achieved in the last 5 years equivalent to requirement of 19,280 households.

Moreover, RWH facility is available at different plants of M&M that includes Swaraj Division Plant 1 and Kandivali & Zaheerabad plant. These plants achieved the following milestones:

- Recycling and reusing of ETP water in process
- Water consumption reduction in new paint line
- Water footprint reduction: 28 per cent
- SD: 42 per cent compared to FY2016–2017
- Automotive sector and farm equipment sector recycled and reused 35 per cent and 43 per cent, respectively

The total hazardous waste generated in FY2017–2018 was 3,695 MT, of which 1,922 MT was recycled.

In October 2016, M&M became the first Indian company to launch an internal carbon price of $10 per metric tonne to reduce the company's carbon footprint and help in meeting its goal of reducing its GHG emission intensity by 25 per cent by 2019 from 2015–2016 levels.

PEOPLE

The Nanhi Kali project has positively impacted the lives of 143,992 underprivileged girls, an increase of 10 per cent from 2016–2017.

Under CSR investment, 143,992 girls were supported under Nanhi Kali programme. In addition to that, 10,007 adolescent girls were supported through the N Star Life Skills centres.

Under livelihood training and placements, 6,323 youth were placed through 'Mahindra Pride Schools', and 41,687 were trained through 'Mahindra Pride Classroom model'.

Under the public health program, 7,641 people received medical and diagnostics services through the 'Lifeline Express' at Ratlam Rural Development. Total 751 farmers from 79 villages in Wardha, Maharashtra, were benefited from the comprehensive agrarian solutions offered through the Wardha Farmer Family Project.

More than 25,000 people across the company adopted *LED* lights, energy-efficient fans, energy-efficient ACs and aerators for taps. Many employees took steps to reduce their energy consumption at home and participated in campaigns run by the company.

The Mahindra Group crossed ₹2 trillion in market capitalization during the year. M&M + MVML recorded an increase of 15 per cent in net sales and operating income of ₹475.77 billion in the year under review as against ₹413.78 billion in the previous year. In the farm sector, their market share (including Gromax) for the FY stood at 42.9 per cent. It was the highest ever market share for them, and they maintained the leading position of the domestic tractor market for the 35th consecutive year. Growth in earnings per share (basic) was 19.4 per cent compared to ₹36.64 in FY2018 (M&M Ltd.)

Surge in profit after tax before EI 23.4 per cent and 15 per cent increase in the top line.

ROCE 19.6 per cent up 270 bps

Dividend (proposed) ₹7.5

Increase in market capitalization 115 times

35,265 people benefited from the integrated watershed management programme in 48 villages in Bhopal and Haryana, resulting in increased agricultural productivity and improved living standards.

Profit

There was an saving of 14 lakh units of energy per annum costing approximate of ₹1 crore, moreover, it helped in carbon reduction of 1,167 tonnes.

As per FY2017–2018, over the last two years, total water consumption has come down by almost 134,696 cu. m.

Automotive sector and farm equipment sector recycled and reused 35 per cent and 43 per cent, respectively, of the total water consumed. In addition, the quantum of renewable energy in the energy basket jumped from 3,909 MWh in the previous year to 8,972 MWh this year, an increase of over 100 per cent.

The solar plant was installed with 269 kWp at a tractor warehouse with a catering capacity of 27 per cent of the power requirement in the Jaipur plant. Against the target of 477,947 MWh set for FY2017–2018, the total energy consumed stood at 473,132 MWh. Energy generated or purchased from renewable energy sources, such as wind and solar, saw a significant increase of over 100 per cent in the total energy consumed to 8,972 MWh from 3,909 MWh, due to an increase in solar and wind capacities at their plants.

CSR contributions stood at ₹81.97 crore in FY2017–2018 with a focus on girl child, youth and farmers in the domains of education, health and the environment.

In FY2016–2017, 498,919 cu. m of water was recycled and reused across businesses. Total 35 per cent of the total water consumption was recycled and reused. Total net freshwater consumption for FY2017–2018 stood at 1.373145 million cubic metres, as against the set target of 1.5116 million cubic metres. At M&M, the material consumption of semi-manufactured material (tonnes) came down by 4.1 per cent to 762,121 tonnes, compared to last year's 794,717 tonnes. Consumption of semi-manufactured material (liquid) also decreased by over 52 per cent to 3,886 kl compared to previous year's 8,139 kl.

Source: Annual report and sustainability reporting of M&M.[5]

ITC: Sustainable Societal Value

ITC predominantly has an objective to create societal value while working in sustainable way.

Thus, the company tries to manifest this in a number of ways. Economic activities in rural areas are targeted towards economic empowerment with various capacity-building programmes to ensure that CSR initiatives for disadvantaged groups in society are of assistance to them. The company also believes in the TBL principle and is inspired by the fact that the company has it with the tag line 'Sab Saath Badhein'.

The company believes that an effective stakeholder engagement process is required for achieving its sustainability goal. The approach focuses on the inclusive growth perspective.

From top to bottom, the policies towards EHS are aligned.

Life cycle sustainability and responsible sourcing is the framework that is followed in the company. The company ensures

---

[5] https://www.mahindra.com/resources/pdf/sustainability/Mahindra-Sustainability-Report-2018-19.pdf

that the entire supply chain must be covered under this process with time.

For achieving this, the company in the hospitality industry took the first mover advantage. It assessed consumers' preferences and understanding, and it was derived that sustainability can be a competitive advantage to the company if it is able to provide services based on consumer preferences, it can definitely give an edge over others. Also, large consumers will focus more on buying products and services of companies that focus on TBL. The company puts efforts to create widespread awareness about the TBL approach. The creative director, Piyush Pandey, mentioned that the campaign would throw light on ITC's way of doing business in creating value, not as a charity, but preferably amalgamating it as a sustainable way of doing business. The campaign would focus on initiatives in watershed development, afforestation and social forestry and the e-Choupal network of connecting farmers.

ITC is the only company in the world of comparable dimension to be carbon positive for 13 years, water positive for 16 years and solid waste recycling positive for 11 years, apart from generating livelihoods for over six million people and, while integrating this idea of campaign, it would be large-scale sustainability interventions for Indian companies.

Moreover, six units of ITC have more than 90 per cent of their electrical energy requirements from renewable sources by FY2017–2018.

The area which is under forest cover is approximately 683,423 acres.

Total 63,403 acres of plantation were added under Social and Farm Forestry Initiatives (as on 31 March 2018). The company has measured that the initiative could grab 5,458,077 tonnes of CO_2.

PROFIT

₹2.91 billion was spent on CSR activities in 2018 at ITC.

In 2017, the consumption of 'renewable energy' was 43.2 per cent.

Total 1,599 kilo tonnes CO_2 was the total GHG emissions in 2017, which excludes biogenic emissions = Scope 1 + Scope 2 + Scope 3.

In which, Scope 1 is direct GHG emissions (kilo tonnes CO_2e)

Scope 2 is indirect GHG emissions (kilo tonnes CO_2e)

Scope 3 is other indirect GHG emissions (kilo tonnes CO_2e).

A total of 865 kilo tonnes CO_2 biogenic emissions were experienced in 2017 at ITC. Although a dip was also contributed owing to the shutdown of a soda recovery boiler.

In 2017, under the air emission category, SO_2 was 889 tonnes, NOx was 808 tonnes, and particulate matter was 609 tonnes.

Under water intake category by the company treated effluent discharge was 23.57 million kilo litre, total RWH potential was 33.07 million kilo litre (It includes RWH potential created within ITC units + RWH potential created through watershed projects cumulative for that year).

Under the waste management category, total waste generated was 725,095 tonnes, which was higher than the previous year due to ITC's inclusion of new units in the reporting boundary and the commissioning of the bleached chemical thermomechanical pulp mill at the Bhadrachalam Unit of Paperboards and Specialty Paper Business.

Total 43.2 per cent of ITC's overall energy requirement is met by green energy.

Source: Annual report and sustainability reporting of ITC.[6]

---

[6] https://www.itcportal.com/sustainability/sustainabilty-reports.aspx

Marriott International

In most of the hotels, Marriot International has installed low-carbon or renewable energy systems, such as geothermal, wind and solar. For example, 21 Marriott properties in India harness 37 per cent of their electricity needs from local wind and solar sources. In 2016, a 536-kilowatt solar photovoltaic system was installed on the rooftop of the Anaheim Marriott in California. Marriott's water conservation initiatives target specific aspects of hotel operations, including laundry and linen/terry reuse programmes, dishwashing and water facilities at restaurants and events, central plant operations; landscaping/irrigation and golf course maintenance/operation.

BENEFITS OF TRIPLE BOTTOM LINE

The organization has benefited a lot from the TBL concept and has driven change in various ways such as follows:

- From top to bottom and at all levels, ethics and corporate governance are in place in the organization.

- Culture that is value driven is ensured at all levels.

- Systems such as performance monitoring and risk management must be sound and well in place.

- Results in enhancement of formal systems and better communication with key stakeholders such as the finance sector, suppliers, the community and customers.

- Value-driven, environmentally aware and conscious staff is in place.

- Staff is more competent and has better skill sets.

- Employees in general are performance driven.

- Work values and professionalism are better in the new set of employees.

- Benchmarking practices within the industry are more followed.

- Employees follow team spirit.

- Retention and long-term stay of employees in these organizations.

- Better company reputation globally.

- All of these practices will result in better growth opportunities available to these companies.

- All of these benefits will give positive results in terms of increased market share.

In addition, its adoption aids in enhancing governance mechanisms in the organization, along with prioritizing non-economic measures to gauge the success of the firm. It helps instiling values that uphold social and environmental factors in assessing the organization's culture. It sends a strong signal to markets conveying to customers and stakeholders how the organization has a holistic approach in managing its operations. Organizations that have implemented the TBL approach have recorded better market valuation over time (Goel, 2013).

Do you know of the recent responsible business practices of listed companies in India?

Read more at https://www.sebi.gov.in/legal/circulars/nov-2015/format-for-business-responsibility-report-brr-_30954.html

TRIPLE BOTTOM LINE/SUSTAINABILITY REPORTING

For attaining the concept of SD, popularly known as TBL, it is expected that the organization should not only be able to assess its practices but should also be able to disclose them to its internal stakeholders as well as to its external stakeholders. These practices must be aligned with the organization's strategic objectives towards the achievement of SD. This is actually a broad term and encompasses all three aspects of economic, environmental and social performance.

ENHANCING TBL REPORTING IN INDIA

Although when we see the guidelines issued by the government and the requirement to society as a whole that it is an urgent matter and needs to be followed at every level, practically, the execution of such guidelines is not very appealing and there are various inconsistencies at each and every level.

We, as an educated and informed citizen, understand the importance and urgency of it, but unfortunately it is not followed in that manner. Reporting is expected but not mandatory for small- and medium-sized enterprises, and thus these small organizations, in particular, are not even assessing and disclosing such practices (India Inc.). The reason may be either that they do not bother or they know that there is no legal enforcement on non-compliance or they do not have adequate tools and knowledge so that they can adhere to such principles while producing a product or service.

Moreover, the analysis derived here shows that there are two major factors that are the reasons of non-compliance: first, is the sustainability reporting-related practice that is feasible but not yet available in a very concrete way? Policymakers and advocates themselves struggle with aspects as how it can be implemented in a universal manner. Moreover, there is no uniformity and less standardization in terms of measures, codes or guiding principles.

The second issue comes with the parameters suggested for sustainable reporting. These metrics are more or less subjective in nature. In the absence of clear and straightforward evaluation metrics, it is trapped under the approach of qualitative reporting. This gives a lot of space to ambiguity. The diversity content contributes it further with less scope to to dive further. Moreover, best practices and models can be used as a guide by others in the future course of action.

These issues are important and need special attention for making the TBL process a success in the general term.

REFERENCES

Elkington, J. (2013). Enter the triple bottom line. In A. Henriques & J. Richardson (Eds.), *The triple bottom line* (pp. 23–38). Routledge.

Goel, P. (2010). Triple bottom line reporting: An analytical approach for corporate sustainability. *Journal of Finance, Accounting & Management*, *1*(1), 27.

Vanclay, F. (2004). Impact assessment and the triple bottom line: Competing pathways to sustainability. In *Sustainability and Social Science Round Table Proceedings*, *2003*, University of Technology.

SUGGESTED READINGS

Alhaddi, H. (2015). Triple bottom line and sustainability: A literature review. *Business and Management Studies*, *1*(2), 6–10.

Climate Disclosure Standards Board. (2018). The reporting exchange: Sustainability reporting landscape in India. https://

www.cdsb.net/sites/default/files/sustainability_india_report_web.pdf

Gajwani, A. (2019). The new balance sheet: Life beyond profits. *Livemint*. https://www.livemint.com/news/india/the-newbalance-sheet-life-beyond-profits-1557664657294.html

https://www.globalreporting.org/information/news-and-press-center/Pages/Leading-Indian-companies-join-GRI%27s-reporting-network.aspx

//economictimes.indiatimes.com/articleshow/62513622.cms?utm_source=contentofinterest&utm_medium=text&utm_campaign=cppst

//economictimes.indiatimes.com/articleshow/62513622.cms?utm_source=contentofinterest&utm_medium=text&utm_campaign=cppst

https://www.marutisuzuki.com/corporate/about-us/sustainability

http://annualreview.larsentoubro.com/corporate-social-responsibility.html

https://www.itcportal.com/sustainability/sustainabilty-reports.aspx

https://www.pcblltd.com/pcbl-sustainability-review-2018/

http://serve360.marriott.com/wp-content/uploads/2019/09/2019_Serve_360_Report.pdf

https://www.globalreporting.org/information/news-and-press-center/Pages/Leading-Indian-companies-join-GRI%27s-reporting-network.aspx

EMPLOYEE'S INITIATIVES AND PERSPECTIVE

Ramesh, a 35-year-old employee working in IT has switched his job last month. The idea behind switching job was better learning opportunity along with a generous pay hike. Joining a new organization gave Ramesh a completely new perspective on how an organization can be run. The pervious employers focused on the bottom line, clients and market share but SCS Ltd was a very environment driven organization. Ramesh can remember the very first day in office, as soon as he had stepped inside the office building, he could sense how important sustainability was for his new employer. Right near the reception he could see a wall adorning the mission statement of SCS Ltd which clearly mandated that EM was important and the organization was committed to the principles of Triple P bottom line in which organizations put emphasis on PPP. His induction training included a session with the sustainability head of the organization in which the head not only talked about the sustainability goals the organization had set for the next five years but also talked about how the organization expected employees in all the departments to think about the environmental implications of their actions. In fact, for every new business project there was a format given which was supposed to disclose the environmental impact of each of the new initiatives.

The head also discussed a number of environmental training programmes the employees were supposed to attend. Although IT is not supposed to be a polluting industry, the organization aspired to become a 'zero carbon emission' facility over the next five years. Ramesh had also spotted a number of his colleagues wearing a badge that said 'I am an environment enthusiast'. Apparently, such badges were like badges of honour in the organization given to employees who had given suggestions to improve sustainability in SCS Ltd along with a gift voucher. Employees had given great ideas to make the workplace green such as having plants on desks and sidewalks, banishing plastic bottles in meetings and employees bringing their own cups and cutlery instead of using the disposable ones in the office. The organization also had an employee-driven car-pooling programme and employees took turns in bringing their vehicles out on the road. Ramesh for the first time could see how involved and committed the employees were in promoting sustainability in SCS Ltd.

GREEN BEHAVIOUR A GOOD THING!

Employees as individuals may demonstrate environmental behaviours in many forms that range from activism (taking up environmental causes on their own), non-activist in the public domain (green purchasing), private domain pro-environmental behaviour (waste segregation and energy conservation at home) and pro-environmental behaviour at the place of work. Employees' pro-environmental behaviour or green behaviour simply put would imply the voluntary engagement of employees in the organizational green initiatives.

One form of green behaviour would be the in-role green behaviour in which the employees may take care of resource conservation while performing their tasks. The other form of pro-environmental behaviour would involve employees' initiatives that could be a form of extra-role behaviour in which the employees can participate in suggestion schemes and attempt to tweak existing processes to make them environment friendly. This may also include spreading environmental awareness among colleagues, customers and the community at large.

EMPLOYEES PLAY A PIVOTAL ROLE IN GREENING OF THE WORKSPACE

Harsh as an engineer working in a factory manufacturing industrial batteries was very impressed with the organization's commitment to quality, cleanliness and EM. One of the best things about all the employee initiatives at the plant was the involvement of everyone working there. In a remarkable employee initiative, which involved a group of sweepers, the employees worked together to treat and manage the effluents discharged in the factory. They gave suggestions to slightly change the way in which waste disposal was taking place leading to the saving of reusable chemicals and discharge of cleaner and less hazardous waste. The minor changes in the processes led to considerable annual savings. The group also made presentations to the top management and visitors who came to study and benchmark best practices in the factory. What was interesting was the encouragement given to the group and the belief that good ideas can come from anywhere in the plant. This widely celebrated story motivated other workmen to suggest changes in their work processes. Harsh realized that big expensive technological changes are not the only means of improving environmental condition. The cumulative effects of employees' suggestions not only helped to make the organization sustainable but also made employees take pride in their work.

As the narrative suggests, if an organization wants to adopt the strategy of sustainability, it has to make sure that employees at all levels in their respective roles need to be environment conscious. Employees' green behaviour has a positive impact on the organization's environmental outcomes in terms of reduction in resource inefficiencies and cost. EI in eco-innovations can help the organization gain competitive advantage. Employees may contribute to organizational sustainability by reducing energy usage, curbing pollutants, bringing more efficiency to the organization's EM architecture, making suggestions for reducing environmental footprints through reuse and recycling and contribution to eco-innovations in products and processes. Some examples of daily pro-environmental behaviour could be switching off lights while leaving office, using double-sided printing, discouraging usage of disposable cups and PET water bottles, using teleconferencing instead of travelling to meeting venues, using eco-friendly forms of commuting like cycling or carpooling and printing drafts on the discarded sheets of paper.

It is interesting to note that employees at a personal level may be demonstrating pro-environmental behaviour but may not find the climate to be environmentally conducive in the organization. Behaviour in non work situations very often does not spill over into the work setting. Employees may feel better motivated to be environmentally conscious at home than at the place of work. The employees do not get individualized energy bills at work to keep a tab on energy consumption, which may result in wastage as nobody is individually accountable for the usage. Very often, they have to share resources and equipment with others taking away control over usage. Sometimes when employees suggest small changes to save resources to their peers, they may face a lot of resistance as the peers may not see the immediate environmental benefits of changes. An employee was also labelled the 'green terrorist' in the organization for suggesting changes to make the processes green. Hence, employees may experience some inhibitors while taking actions on their own. Sometimes, an employee may also be in a dilemma to choose between an environmentally appropriate action and an action that gives immediate economic results. Until now organizations have not mandated environmentally responsible behaviour in job roles, hence, when employees take environmental actions, such behaviours are clustered in the domain of extra-role behaviours or organizational citizenship behaviour. Organizations definitely recognize and appreciate such behaviours, but, unfortunately, sporadic reinforcement using prizes and gifts by the organizations does not inculcate a sense of responsibility and accountability among employees to practise such behaviour on a regular basis. The employees are not motivated to make pro-environmental choices as a permanent part of their routine work behaviour.

Employees' pro-environmental behaviour is influenced by personal as well as organizational factors. At the personal level, the employee's personality and motivation can impact the degree of involvement in green initiatives. The organization-level factors such as policies, organizational culture and leadership behaviour can promote employee green behaviour.

People who have green values may be attracted to join organizations that value the environment, and they would be the ones to champion green efforts in organizations. One such story is of Kanika Kapila who was a chemical engineering student at the University of Calgary. She happened to participate in Schneider Electric's 'Go Green' global student challenge. She along with her team prepared a project on recycling of greenhouse gas emissions from power plants into usable products. Her project not only got shortlisted for the finals, but she was also invited to visit the organization and interact with the employees. She may not have won the competition, but her potential earned her a job at Schneider Electric. This was a perfect fit between the environmental passion she had with the organization's commitment to sustainability.[1] Thus, the employee's environmental disposition will work in favour of

---

[1] https://blog.se.com/life-at-schneider-electric/2019/04/17/from-go-green-finalist-to-schneider-electric-employee/

the organization and it will also act as a motivating factor for the employees who will find a channel to work on initiatives which they value. Employees who have pro-environmental attitudes are more conscious of the impact of their actions and, hence, show higher willingness to participate in the organization's environmental projects and actions. Managers with pro-environmental attitudes are more inclined to execute environment projects. Employees with positive affect, that is, feeling excited and enthusiastic would also show enthusiasm in demonstrating pro-environmental attitudes. Research suggests that employees who have pro-environmental values will be more inclined to demonstrate green behaviour. The values which make the individual prefer actions that save or conserve the environment will only be demonstrated if the organization provides a conducive space for green behaviour to emerge. Researchers have tried to account for pro-environmental behaviour among employees in terms of sympathy for others, emotional affinity towards nature and empathy for wild animals. Some religious beliefs which propagate nature as divine are also responsible for individual's pro-environmental actions. Employee's pro-social values or altruistic motives which make people think about others also act as influencers.

●—●●●●●●●●●●—●

Swati works for an advertising firm and one of her colleagues has started the waste collection project in office. All employees are supposed to dump wet and dry waste separately in bins earmarked for them and the office has done away with the waste bins kept next to each cubicle. Swati has to walk to dump the waste and this sometimes becomes irritating. But at the end of each month she finds some data shared on waste management by the company. She does realize that collectively employees generate a lot of waste that can be handled better.

After the new creative director joined, who is very passionate about green matters, the number of printers were reduced in the office. Initially, it was difficult for Swati not to see how her ideas and designs look on paper, but she is gradually getting accustomed to the change. In the last Environment Day celebrations, the organization had a brainstorming session on how the employees can adopt green behaviour and the team had come up with a list of 10 environmentally desirable behaviours. This was then shared with all the employees and a checklist was placed in each cubicle to help employees keep track of their behaviour. The organization has also devised a rubric to measure resource consumption in the office such as electricity, paper and water and it shares those figures on a weekly basis. The organization is planning to seek nominations for one of the sustainability awards this year and all the employees are mighty thrilled about it.

Very often, pro-environmental behaviour may make people put in extra effort without gaining any immediate gratification. Employees will indulge in that behaviour provided they see some environmental gain from it. The organizations can influence employees by signalling the organization's green intent via its mission statement, pro-environmental programmes and policies. Also, changing the context at the workplace, for example, displaying pro-environmental messages, initiating waste segregation, promoting use of electric vehicles and other such initiatives may work well for employees who are already environmentally inclined.

Do you know how Central Pollution Control Board (CPCB) in

India helps in managing pollution?

Read more at https://www.india.gov.in/official-website-central-pollution-control-board

HOW ORGANIZATIONS CAN MOTIVATE PRO-ENVIRONMENTAL BEHAVIOUR?

Organizations need to promote a green-oriented culture which would be a signal to the employees that green actions and ideas are encouraged in the organization. The presence of sustainability policy and green climate in the organization works in favour of employee's pro-environmental behaviour. Organizations need to have a mix of sustainability projects that are high impact as well as smaller short-term projects which would keep the momentum going on the environmental front. The high impact projects involve changes in behaviours, routines and work and, hence, are more difficult to implement. The smaller sustainability initiatives will have higher ownership in the employee group as the initiatives would mostly be employee driven and this would go a long way in institutionalizing green culture in the organization.

Leader's Influence

Another very important influencer for promoting employee initiatives is the leader's behaviour. By launching environmental projects, the leader demonstrates environmental consciousness as well as the seriousness of the organization in protecting the environment. The leader acts as the role model and inspires the employees to participate in such programmes. Leader's actions and the peers' focus on green behaviour act as important motivators for individual employees to take up green workplace behaviour. It is seen that merely formulating an environmental policy and employee participation forums does not necessarily elicit positive response from the employees. The leaders can encourage employees by expressing their own commitment to environmental causes and getting involved in activities that promote the greening of the organization.

Successful Employee Pro-environmental Behaviour Narratives

Many a time, even a single person can take initiatives that can make a huge difference to the organization's sustainability efforts. There are several inspiring stories of individuals who took up sustainability even before it became popular.

Energy-saving Behaviour Awarded

One such person being David Hunag, who was a facilities manager for a US-based organization. He noticed the after-hours wastage of energy in the facility where equipment was not turned off after work hours. He brought this to the management's notice and the organization kick-started energy conservation projects. Huang's energy saving measures won him an award and audience with the senior manager in charge of sustainability where he could discuss his sustainability ideas. His single-handed efforts made the company take energy conservation seriously by setting targets for all its facilities. The energy savings were incentivized by connecting them with the bonus of the managers.

Special Sustainability Initiative for Employees

Organizations run special sustainability programmes for employees. Symantec organizes the 'Going Green' campaign exclusively for employees which have given great ideas on use of recyclable water bottles, riding bicycles to work and planting trees. Such initiatives go a long way in demonstrating that employees have a big impact on an organization's sustainability efforts.[2]

---

[2] https://www.caelusgreenroom.com/going-green-for-a-more-sustainable-business-and-future/

One's efforts pave the way to carbon neutrality. Another inspiring story is of Valerie Mac-Seing who happens to be a lawyer based in Montreal. When she took the initiative to discard plastic from the office kitchen and paper towels, there was a lot of protests from her senior colleagues, but she soldiered on. Her contemporaries saw some merit in her efforts and joined her green committee. Today, there has been a turnaround in the organization's environmental philosophy and the firm is proud of what she did as it has become the first law firm to be declared carbon neutral. Good sustainability related ideas have mostly come from the employees closest to the operations. Organizations need to provide a platform for them to showcase those ideas.

There are occasions when the peers have shown support for the green champions. When an employee wanted to take the initiative of recycling soda cans that she had been stocking but doing it alone seemed to be formidable, she checked with her colleagues, and found that they were keen to join her and become a part of the recycling project. In another instance, a manager could influence her colleagues and other employees to give green gifts and helped them by preparing and sharing a database of vendors selling green products.

Support Employees' Ideas!

Employees have a much better understanding of work processes and they are in a better position to suggest changes. Organizations have to take those ideas forward. There are stories of organizations providing enormous support for employees' ideas. For environmentally conscious organizations, employees agree that when they come up with green ideas, their employers provide support. One such company is Lush. It manufactures handmade soaps. Several employee initiatives that they implemented were holding an interdepartmental competition to reduce consumption of energy, starting a garden adjacent to their facility and a composting unit to divert wastes to landfills. They have also created a position for green officer who can systematically continue such efforts.

Decentralize the Sustainability Drive: Give Space to Be Sustainably Creative

Organizations have to give enough autonomy to employees to drive the organization's sustainability initiatives. ISL Engineering and Land Services allowed its employees who were environment conscious to use 10 per cent of the office time to plan and implement environmental projects, attend environmental events and network with green partners. Employees are very engaged as environmental conservation has changed domains from being extra-role to intra-role in the organization. They have not only worked for the betterment of the organization, but they also intend to help their customers in becoming green too.

Employees Can Successfully Drive Sustainability

Another interesting example is of Intuit which has employee-championed environmental programmes and processes. The organization has green teams that volunteer for community projects such as clean-up of river valley parkland, organizing riding of bikes to generate pedal power for generators which can operate sound systems and kitchen blenders, work in community gardens, join in fruit picking and distribution of fruits and vegetables to the needy in the neighbourhood. The organization does not decide which activities are to be initiated, it is all employee driven. Intuit has understood that a bottom-up approach is far more effective than a top-down approach. Giving a free hand to the employees has earned the company credibility and employee engagement in the environmental programmes.

Employees Know What Is Best

Being closest to operations employees can offer practical ideas for resource conservation and cost savings and ideas for better community development. In the case of Unilever tea factory on Trafford Park, workers came up with a great idea of shortening the end seals of teabags by a few millimetres leading to enormous savings in paper and costs. At the Khamgaon factory of Unilever, workers came up with the idea of setting up a centre for training in beauty and hair care to help the women in the neighbouring community to work as make-up professionals or start their own ventures.

-●●●●●●●●●●●-

Karan has always been very passionate about environmental issues, and he has a strong belief that everyone needs to be environmentally conscious to make a difference to this planet. He has been an inquisitive child and would spend a lot of time searching for information about environment and sustainability. He had not only planted a number of trees surrounding his house but also helped neighbours in making their backyards green. He would get very angry and upset when he would find people wasting paper, water and electricity and try and make them see how their small actions were contributing to environmental degradation. This passion made him join an NGO that worked towards increasing environmental awareness. Karan's enthusiasm and friendliness would help him in giving talks on EM. When it was time for him to begin his corporate career after his postgraduation, he visited the websites of the prospective employers to check their stance on environment and sustainability. His firm belief was that he will not be involved with an organization which did not care about the environment. Fortunately, one of the organizations that came to the campus was among the top 10 sustainable organizations in India. His decision to join the organization was driven by not only the role but the matching of his environmental values with those of the organization.

It can be seen that pro-environmental behaviour is influenced by employees' environmental pre-disposition, biospheric values (which imply a concern 'for the welfare of those in larger society and world and for nature', as defined by Schwartz) and personality traits which make them look after others and the society at large. An organization can screen employees for their environmental orientation at the time of employee selection. It can also attract such employees by having sustainability as its employer value proposition. Once the organization attracts talent that is environmentally responsible, it needs to support employee initiatives and efforts to make the organization and the world a better place. Organizations need to inculcate environmental responsibility among the employees in such a way that they would be environmentally conscious in all that they do. In the words of the head of manufacturing at PCBL,

> we not only believe in following green initiatives when we are at workplace, but it is so obvious now with us that even after leaving the workplace the importance of saving the resources and motivating others for the same remains with us. And, we really feel proud that we are involved in the great cause.[3]

SUGGESTED READINGS

Bamberg, S., & Möser, G. (2007). Twenty years after Hines, Hungerford, and Tomera: A new meta-analysis of psycho-social determinants of pro-environmental behaviour. *Journal of Environmental Psychology*, *27*(1), 14–25.

---

[3] Source: Interview conducted by the authors

Bissing-Olson, M. J., Iyer, A., Fielding, K. S., & Zacher, H. (2013). Relationships between daily affect and pro-environmental behavior at work: The moderating role of pro-environmental attitude. *Journal of Organizational Behavior, 34*(2), 156–175.

Boiral, O., Paillé, P., & Raineri, N. (2015). The nature of employees' pro-environmental behaviors. In J. L. Robertson & J. Barling (Eds.), *The psychology of green organizations* (12–32). Oxford University Press.

Buhl, A., Blazejewski, S., & Dittmer, F. (2016). The more, the merrier: Why and how employee-driven eco-innovation enhances environmental and competitive advantage. *Sustainability, 8*(9), 946.

Chou, C. J. (2014). Hotels' environmental policies and employee personal environmental beliefs: Interactions and outcomes. *Tourism Management, 40,* 436–446.

Kim, A., Kim, Y., Han, K., Jackson, S. E., & Ployhart, R. E. (2017). Multilevel influences on voluntary workplace green behavior: Individual differences, leader behavior, and coworker advocacy. *Journal of Management, 43*(5), 1335–1358.

Littleford, C., Ryley, T. J., & Firth, S. K. (2014). Context, control and the spillover of energy use behaviours between office and home settings. *Journal of Environmental Psychology, 40,* 157–166.

Martin, C., & Czellar, S. (2017). Where do biospheric values come from? A connectedness to nature perspective. *Journal of Environmental Psychology, 52,* 56–68.

Norton, T. A., Zacher, H., & Ashkanasy, N. M. (2014). Organisational sustainability policies and employee green behaviour: The mediating role of work climate perceptions. *Journal of Environmental Psychology, 38,* 49–54.

Ones, D. S., & Dilchert, S. (2012). Employee green behaviors. In Jackson, S. E., Ones, D. S., & Dilchert, S. (Eds.), *Managing human resources for environmental sustainability* (85–116). Jossey-Bass/Wiley.

Paillé, P., & Boiral, O. (2013). Pro-environmental behavior at work: Construct validity and determinants. *Journal of Environmental Psychology*, *36*, 118–128.

Ramus, C. A. (2001). Organizational support for employees: Encouraging creative ideas for environmental sustainability. *California Management Review*, *43*(3), 85–105.

Ruepert, A. M., Keizer, K., & Steg, L. (2017). The relationship between corporate environmental responsibility, employees' biospheric values and pro-environmental behaviour at work. *Journal of Environmental Psychology*, *54*, 65–78.

Saeed, B. B., Afsar, B., Hafeez, S., Khan, I., Tahir, M., & Afridi, M. A. (2019). Promoting employee's proenvironmental behavior through green human resource management practices. *Corporate Social Responsibility and Environmental Management*, *26*(2), 424–438.

Unsworth, K. L., Dmitrieva, A., & Adriasola, E. (2013). Changing behaviour: Increasing the effectiveness of workplace interventions in creating pro-environmental behaviour change. *Journal of Organizational Behavior*, *34*(2), 211–229.

Wesselink, R., Blok, V., & Ringersma, J. (2017). Pro-environmental behaviour in the workplace and the role of managers and organisation. *Journal of Cleaner Production*, *168*, 1679–1687.

Zientara, P., & Zamojska, A. (2018). Green organizational climates and employee pro-environmental behaviour in the hotel industry. *Journal of Sustainable Tourism*, *26*(7), 1142–1159.

A GREENER FUTURE

> *The greatest challenges humans face throughout their lives are two: the challenge of where to start and the challenge of when to stop.*
>
> **Sameh Elsayed**

Although sustainability efforts have gained momentum in the last decade, there is a need for nations and organizations to accelerate the efforts. The need for sustainable practices is going to be of paramount importance in the years to come. As the nations have committed meeting United Nations SDGs by 2050, conserving energy, reducing wastage of water and commitment to responsible production and consumption becomes every citizen's responsibility. Many countries have already set tangible targets for meeting the 2050 goals.

Experts have always warned people about the impacts of climate change, global warming and the onset of a pandemic (recent example, COVID-19) can completely rewire people's brains. All these environmental changes will have far reaching impact on humanity and life on the planet. The threat of annihilation of life from the planet due to exhaustion of consumable resources does not seem to be an empty threat, rather it is a reality waiting to unfold over the next few decades. It is the responsibility of every human being to save the planet and the resources for the future generations. The travel and rehabilitation on a different planet is still a fantasy but the need to save the planet is a hard reality. Individuals, nations and corporations need to do their bit to ensure that the planet is safe, and life is secure.

Here, we mean each stakeholder, be it governments or organizations or employees, needs to take the responsibility of contributing for the common good. The discussion on what the harm we have already created, what presently we are doing and what needs to be done needs to be comprehended by each and everyone.

One can learn from the best practices. One can also learn from the mistakes. Thus, the chapter is committed for reiterating what is already said and what we really need to learn and what needs to be done for the future.

In an organization, the success of product or service depends on how much the company has invested involving all the stakeholders in the process, and how much they feel committed to achieve the same.

Do you know how Global Reporting Initiative is helping companies towards achieving the goals of environment and sustainability?

Read more at https://www.globalreporting.org/Pages/default.aspx

CIRCULAR ECONOMY

There is a lot of talk on circular economy—it is expected from organizations that they calibrate recycling mechanisms in the design of their products. A circular design implies a product design that considers the environmental implications throughout the product life cycle from the cradle to the grave. The design should entail optimum resource usage in manufacturing as well as in decomposition, recycling and repurposing of the discards after usage of the product. This provision has been included in what is called 'extended producer's responsibility (EPR)' and in the future, more and more organizations would be expected to take responsibility for the end outcome of their products. This would involve organizations in the waste management process of their products. Electronics companies and computer manufacturing organizations have already started to discharge EPR by collecting e-wastes form customers and taking care of the recycling, disposal or repurposing.

The factories of the future are also being envisaged as that would exist in complete harmony with nature and would employ technologies that emit no carbon footprint and be beneficial for the adjoining localities. Such establishments instead of exploiting resources would work towards harnessing renewable resources of energy and improving water and air quality in the plant and adjacent areas. They would be designed in such a way that they work on PPP methodology, thereby providing doles to all the stakeholders. The architecture, building and resources employed would all be designed to function on the principle that promotes sustainability.

TBL is a systematic, aligned and inclusive effort. HR in this needs to come up with new ideas and practices that are feasible while working in the organization. The process may be related to, that is, recruitment and selection, hiring, training, developing, compensating, evaluating performance and so on. Employees need to adhere to them for having better outcome.

In the GRI study on 'Sustainability and Reporting Trends 2025', experts and practitioners presented that it is highly expected that organizations need to take better care and more responsibility for solving environmental difficulties. Organizations need to understand the environmental challenges, and how they affect businesses. Thus, the organizations must derive innovative solutions for the same. The establishments must have actionable clear goals and have to partner with the important actors in the ecosystem to combat the environmental and sustainability related challenges. Industrial bodies, as per the GRI study, would need to be more transparent in sharing their sustainability information and try to experiment with sustainable business models. The emphasis must be on developing new sustainability linked metric and digital reporting on environmental performance on real-time basis.

STAKEHOLDERS' ROLE

External stakeholders, that is, customers and regulators and internal stakeholders, that is, HR management teams, top and middle managers or all the employees can influence the overall value chain in the systems and processes. Government or industry may constrain organizations in adopting green practices.

In this process, the global awareness is increased, and people become cognizant about the environmental impacts. There is a growing need for organizations to disclose more on their carbon footprints.

In today's time, reporting on sustainability is a choice that organizations make. Reporting platforms follow a voluntary reporting protocol. But in times to come, the reporting on ESG-related matters would become imperative for organizations.

Under ESG, corporations need to measure the sustainability and societal impact of an investment in the organization. All the criteria will be defined, and the comprehensive approach will help in determining the companies' future performance. Organizations, which are concerned for environment and sustainability, are consciously active towards the direction, perceive positive outcomes such as higher profitability, better financial performance and higher stock prices. In addition, customers can also take a bigger responsibility and can trust those companies which apply environmental certification to their products, thus, top management tends to espouse green operations either by averting a penalty or preserving their market share or profitability.

INNOVATION IS THE KEY

Innovative business models for sustainability need to be applied in the organizations to deliver positive results that significantly reduce negative impacts on environment and society. Sustainable business models overpower TBL (PPP) perspective. It is true that the primary objective of an organization is to maximize its financial performance. However, considering only financial performance cannot be the prime motive of an organization. With the heightening of stakeholders' awareness and expectations, there has been a need to employ holistic measures for understanding what can be defined as performance. The argument here is that only financial performance cannot be the indication of a firm's success. Rather, understanding the welfare of employees, who are the source of competitive advantage of the firm, and managing the resources in such a manner that the environmental damage is minimal along with earning profitability is the message here.

Business models help the company in transforming resources into economic value. Business models guide the way that define its competitive strategy by the design of the product or service to its market in an advanced manner. The novelty out of it must be economic feasibility as well. These green pioneering ideas help organizations in the long run. SBM has its influence on a wide range of stakeholders' interests comprising environment and society. The process helps in making changes in the organization's value-network creation in a manner that the delivery of economic values is not much affected. They are crucial in operating and executing corporate innovations that can aid to engrain sustainability for business processes along with gaining the competitive advantage.

DIVERSE PARTNERSHIP

Innovative business models need a diverse partnership. It can be across countries or stakeholders. Government, industry, employees all together can come forward to make the mammoth task happen in a real way. There are plenty of organizations such as WBCSD, UNIDO, the World Bank, UNEP and INGOs which work together in the field of SD to give some of the original ideas. In addition, a number of companies of all sizes across the globe are involved in the noble cause. The corporations try to comply fully with the norms as stipulated by their country's government authorities and innovate in such a manner that without compromising the quality and quantity of product or service, they are able to follow green norms. It is seen that in the process TBL motive is achieved.

As per CPCB, India,

> The country, has a potential and with right choices and the support and proper compliance, large quantum of waste, which is non-recyclable hazardous and other wastes can be segregated. Non-hazardous industrial wastes include plastics wastes, tyre wastes and

non-usable bio-mass. This can be recycled and can be further used as an alternative fuel and raw material (AFR).

SMART ORGANIZATIONS AND GREEN WORKPLACES

Smart organizations know how to ensure core values of their organization. This can happen either by persuading their employees or by giving them a clear message. Organizations like Toyota have demonstrated their unwavering commitment to the environment by institutionalizing the 'Toyota Environmental Challenge 2050' in which the company has set for itself the challenge of zero carbon emission in their vehicles and their manufacturing units by 2050. The commitment is also towards reducing water consumption, improving recycling systems and ensuring development of the society that exists in harmony with nature.

A green workplace is an eco-friendly and focused organization and leans towards the adoption of business practices that are justifiable in nature, energy efficient and well suited to the complex as well as the ever-changing world of business. It is not only green building and green infrastructure, but also it has a much broader scope. It encompasses green competencies, green attitude and green behaviour which are combined synergistically to help the organization become green or sustainable.

Organizations that have made greening a priority for themselves expect environment-centric behaviour from their people and this has resulted in judicious utilization of resources. In addition, consistent assessment of environmental impact while taking business decisions, recycling and repurposing of resources and adoption of sustainable forms of different means are some other important parameters.

Most of the organizations also run employee suggestion schemes for sustainability. Another area in which organizations focus in order to encourage green orientation of employees is providing them environmental training that includes the awareness and green practices followed by the organization. Few companies' examples show that encouraging employees to participate in environmental programmes and eco-initiatives helps organizations in driving their sustainability initiatives.

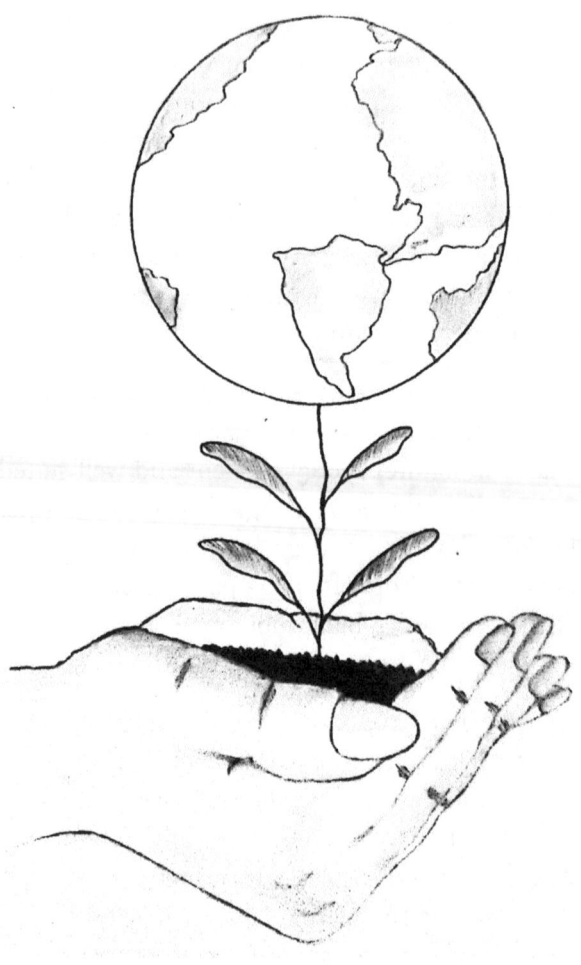

ORGANIZATION'S ROLE: ACTIVE INVOLVEMENT OF LEADERS

The support and assurance for the success of SD and keeping TBL in mind are must. It is applicable from the top management to managers and further to all employees. Considering an organization where the leader is visionary and believes in TBL but fails to communicate with adequate strategy and motivation, the vision thus remains on paper only.

Thus, an inclusive strategy is needed, which has multiple facets. Nowhere the quality of product or service needs to be compromised. Rather, it is an approach that contributes competitive advantage to businesses. It increases employees' satisfaction and retention. It improves the image of the organization globally. It brands itself a place, where people like to work. It becomes the house which can attract talented workforce thus ultimately improves bottom line.

Another scenario in which employees are enthusiastic and want the planet earth to be taken care of with adequate actions and tools. But until and unless top management is supportive or communicates to its stakeholders and adheres to such practices, this many remain a delusion, even though it is in the vision of the organization.

Thus, here the discussion is what actually the role of the stakeholders is, and how much efforts must be drawn. What are the best practices, what are the checks and balances that need to be in place? Unavailability of the alignment of all the pillars may limit the success of a company's sustainability policy. Creating an organizational culture that encourages staff to actively pursue energy-saving, waste-minimization and ethical practices through emotional engagement is needed here.

EMPLOYEE THE DECIDER

Internal stakeholders can initiate green HR initiatives in a bid to attract employees who are environmentally conscious and aware. The managers must lead the way by demonstrating green behaviour. When employees see managers and owners practising conservation, they are more inclined to do it themselves. When each person in a company works together, green business practices become the norm instead of an encumbrance.

Besides, there is growing evidence that graduates prefer working in an organization which values sustainability, thus recruitment of employees is also determined by the sustainability agenda of employers. Moreover, green HR initiatives are viewed as radical changes within an organization and require sufficient time and resources to formulate them into practice. It is seen that organizational enthusiasm may be perceived as operational readiness, financial readiness, staffing readiness, technical readiness as well as knowledge readiness. Aligning all of them is a vital task to happen.

Without commitment from the workforce, the success of a company's sustainability policy is likely to have limited impact. Creating an organizational culture that encourages staff to actively pursue energy-saving, waste-minimization and ethical practices through emotional engagement is key to helping a business reach its sustainability goals.

WHAT GHRM CAN DO: HR IN ACTION

GHRM is the application of HRM policies to encourage the sustainable use of resources within the organization and comprehensively upgrading the practices of environment and sustainability.

GHRM is promptly responsible in creating green workforce that understands, appreciates and applies green initiative and preserves its green objectives throughout the process of recruiting, hiring, training, evaluating, compensating, developing, and advancing the firms' human capital. It denotes policies, practices and systems that make employees of the organization green for the welfare of individual, society and business.

HR needs to ensure that there are adequate green policies available that promote sustainable use of assets within the organization. This becomes the bigger responsibility of HR to create awareness among people about environmental harms. Also, when companies go green, they can save resources without compromising the quality of products or services. Online portals and folders can be created and can be a practice in the organization.

PRACTICAL TIPS

In an organization, employees can be motivated to opt car-pool option or employees can collaborate, living in the similar vicinity, to go to office together. It has multiple benefits. Employees get the opportunity to mingle with each other in a neutral non-office environment. They can share jokes, experiences, learnings and so on. This is a win-win situation. In this way, employees get de-stressed, and there long commuting hours can turn into lots of learnings from each other. Moreover, if the office campus is big, electric cars can be used for commuting from one place to an other. In the campus, there must be proper space for pavements, thus employees, if they wish, can commute on foot for shorter distance.

In the digital era, more emphasis must be given on reducing the burden of paper by creating online folders. Portals that can be used for storing or creating archives of employees' documents, such as, offer letters, CVs, recommendation letters, previous performance records, credentials, etc.

When to Teach

For achieving competitive advantage, companies put lots of efforts in the direction of developing green culture, where they believe that positive outcomes can be achieved with new ways of working. Sustainable way of working is one of those aspects. But for creating the culture of creativity, which can inspire the workforce to think in the manner, needs some thorough planning. Moreover, the change must start from the top. Here, the instance of Mahatma Gandhi is appropriate to mention.

Once a lady went to meet Mahatma Gandhi (an eminent saint from India) along with her son. She was frustrated as her son was having a sweet tooth and was not limiting the intake of consuming *gur* (jaggery) to the optimum level. When Gandhiji met the lady, he listened to her patiently and asked her to come after two weeks. The lady was perplexed and wondered as why Gandhiji is refusing to advise her son now. This was not a great task, it was simply small guidance. Anyway, she visited Gandhiji again after two weeks and this time Gandhiji gave the son wonderful and practical suggestions. That really helped her son in coming out the habit of eating more jaggery. The lady thanked Gandhiji for the advice and support. But out of curiosity, she probed Gandhiji, why had he not counselled her son in the first visit. Gandhiji took a moment and said, 'Ma. When you visited me first, I myself used to eat a lot of gur. First, I trained myself to limit eating gur so that I can give some guidance to your son'.

The story advocates that when employees see leaders practising conservation, they feel inclined to do it more, and the practices become the norm instead of a burden. When we work in an organization, we tend to look to our bosses, the same principle is followed in homes to teach children for good habits and discipline. Parents need to practise self-control first if they want to teach discipline to their wards. The culture of the organization must be the one which encourages and nurtures creative flow of ideas and risks-taking capacity.

Furthermore, the sustainability awareness must be initiated from the one among the employees. During the induction programme itself, employees are to be duly informed about the ethics of the organization, its culture and its ethos and core values, where sustainability is very important. The programme must highlight how the company involved itself in such practices, how it is taking care of things at different levels, how things are managed and what are the final outcomes achieved with them. When employees know the culture and the passion of the organization towards such work, they comprehend it as imperative.

CULTIVATING GREEN CULTURE

EI can be achieved when they actively participate in sustainability related programs of the organization. In addition, the organization needs to empower them so that they feel themselves a part of the organization's green management programme. We all know that employee empowerment always benefits all. When it is applied to environment-related objectives, it helps in limiting environmental damage. It improves productivity and performance. This teaches us how one can learn self-control and gives a lot of scope and space to develop problem-solving skills.

This builds enhanced trust between the management and the employees. Thus, the alignment between employees' skills and capabilities must be such that employees find that they are adding value to the organization's goals. In addition, employees should be given sustainability goals as a part of their KRA. For example, production team can be given some goals that they have to reduce or reserve electricity consumption or water consumption. Or the engineering team can be given the objective to search for a technology/substitute that reduces overall energy or water consumption. Or production team can be given a target to search for replacements that create less harm to the environment. In overall perspective, stakeholders must be communicated to assess the carbon footprints created by their activities and how these carbon emission can be reduced. Moreover, executives should keep themselves informed to find the alternatives that can be used to replace the existing material. Employees must be able to talk freely and share ideas that are for common good.

WORKING IN HARMONY

Working in harmony with nature needs to be promoted. It can start with having an infrastructure available that speaks for itself and values sustainability. Suggestions must be carefully examined and recognized whenever are found to be out of the box idea or actually good to get implemented. Employees who are involved directly in procurement or service have better understanding of the way processes function. If some suggestions come from them, they are actually feasible and carry a lot of value. Moreover, stories of such innovations can be shared internally to motivate the employees further. Employees must be aware that non-compliances of such practices have severe consequences. Thus, the message needs to be clear, straight forward, simple and aligned with all the functions and activities.

Some other ways of motivating employees towards achieving sustainability goals are organizing competitive events where employees submit their innovative ideas for reducing carbon footprints. Or it may be small suggestion schemes for using the alternative sources of energy with a new way of working that actually replaces energy with design.

Moreover, the design thinking approach for reducing the emission or improved way of working can be applied here. To stimulate employees further, incentive schemes can be linked with these ideas or special projects suggested or completed with less usage of resources can be shared as best practice. Another way of inspiring employees can be that employees earn green credits by using personal vehicles less, saving paper, planting trees, participating in community activities and convincing society in general towards environmental consciousness. There can be a system where employees can see the statistics about the company's carbon imprint on the environment, including energy efficiency, paper consumption and recycling. This can encourage the feeling that the efforts put in the direction are not in vain. Employees then can earn even green rewards that may include lifestyle or workplace benefits or giving them some medals or certificates in big company events. Last but not least, emphasis can be given on such activities as promoted by the organization. The events must be seen as full of fun, not just like another stretch goals. Here, employees are required to take the ownership of their activities and they must feel proud of the fact that even a small intervention suggested or implemented by them could make a difference in the lives of millions of people in the coming years.

Before employees can implement green strategies, it would be helpful if they understand how their choices affect company's costs and the environment in the long run, company would like to achieve. The company can involve employees by actively involving their and implementing their suggestions and making them responsible for specific goals like reducing trash or reducing energy consumption.

GREEN TEAM

One more arrangement in the direction is identifying employees who are passionate for green and environment-related aspects. Moreover, while designing a team of green enthusiasts, companies can consciously select persons considering diversity is ensured. Hence, it comprehends employees' representation from all levels, functions/departments and gender. This will give an adequate representation and efforts put by the organization that are easy to communicate and execute at all levels. The message is clear that we need to adhere to environment and sustainability.

It is seen that the efforts of the green culture are reflected beyond the office. Employees make green choices beyond their office space, and their environment sustainability efforts start from their home. For example, it may be a cognizant choice of buying green products and tumbling resources as much as possible.

These small steps taken by employees make them green employees. They are the important resource for the organization and the employees can carry a bigger responsibility in the organization of leading a team for attaining sustainable objectives. Employees feel proud for the work they do. This makes them a better citizen, who has even more energy to drive the team beyond office with lots of conviction.

GO GREEN FROM OFFICE TO HOME

Sustainable Living

Mumbai-based Pappco Greenware produces a wide range of food packaging items including food streamers, paper straws, lunch plates and wooden cones. All the products are eco-friendly and that is the premise on which the company is based on.

The story behind starting a start-up 'Pappco Greenware' is a step to provide environment-friendly goods. The company was started in Mumbai by Anil Agarwal, Aadesh Agarwal and Abhishek Agarwal. They were concerned about the wastage created by food packaging material. Nowadays when we work in offices or when both the couples are working, it is essential for them to order food from outside as they do not have much time available that they can cook all the meals every day. It is seen that mostly office-going individuals, especially working couples, or the bachelors prefer ordering food from outside. The food is packed with disposable materials and thus lots of waste is produced. This includes streamers, lunch plates, food packaging boxes, carry bags and plastic spoons. As per the report of UNEP, 50 per cent of plastic waste generated globally in 2015 was from packaging.

Since 1990, the plastic wastage generation has tripled and the similar case is with plastic production.

The founders of Pappco Greenware learnt that bagasse (sugarcane waste) products can be used as a compostable alternative to plastic. Thus, after some research and by visiting different factories to understand the process, and six months of their continuous effort, resulted in the design of the products that can easily be replaced with eco-friendly stuff. One of the differentiating factors of their product was that they were made of Styrofoam, a biodegradable product. Next challenge was why people should switch to their material over existing one and it was not easy to convince. First, it needed sensitization and awareness about the harms of continuous usage of plastic not only to the planet but to our bodies as well. The constant efforts paid them off, and they could sway a number of organizations in promoting eco-friendly products. Now, in the list of their clients, even Taj Group is included.

Here is the story of designing beautiful products from waste.

Can Waste Be Beautiful?

Nisha runs a workshop for kids in the neighbourhood to teach them to make beautiful handicrafts from household dry waste such as paper and plastic. She began this initiative in order to hook kids' attention towards EM. The message for the kids was that there is some value in waste which could be recycled, reused and repurposed. The children held a small exhibition of the handicrafts they had made and got a lot of praises from the parents and visitors. Nisha thus started inculcating the value among children that they can collect all the paper and plastic at home and can discourage other members of the family from careless dumping. Nisha senses accomplishment as this is the right beginning with young children to an environmental mission towards evolving responsible individuals.

WHAT ONE CAN DO?

Value for Resources

It is right to mention that 'money belongs to us, but resources belong to society'. An example from the rich and high-income country Germany on wasting food products is right to mention here.

The instance happened in Hamburg, Germany, where Anuj (name changed) visited his friend after the office hours at a restaurant. His friend used to work there, thus, to welcome Anuj, his friend threw a small party in the restaurant to welcome his colleagues and friends from India. The restaurant was not big or luxurious but was known for delicious food quality and service. The colleagues placed the order and started chatting. Anuj looked around and saw that there were not many people having food and many tables were empty. He also noticed that there was one young couple celebrating some success. He observed that they have ordered only two dishes and were eating with great love. Anuj was surprised as why only two items on such special occasion. In the meantime, the colleagues of Anuj have ordered few items of different variety considering the preference of all, which seemed like more than what they can actually consume. When the food was served, they started relishing the food. But Anuj noticed that some couples were talking and were pointing to their table. Anuj was surprised, he tried to overhear and found that they were gossiping about them only. The point they were making that these educated persons may waste some food. Anuj was surprised as why others are bothered abut their food order. He was restless and had a small argument with them. One of the old couples called the police, and the cops fined Anuj and their colleagues with 50 euros. They also advised that one should order only as much what one can consume. Anuj and all others felt ashamed. The old lady came near to their table and politely advised that 'in future we may face food crunch or severe crises of basic necessities as food and water. You belong to a country like India where hunger and poverty is a big issue, why you all cannot respect food'.

Source: https://www.moneylife.in/article/penalty-for-wasting-food-can-we-follow-the-german-example/32080.html

---

SAY NO TO HARMFUL CHEMICALS

The usage of plastic for storing food in any form is harmful. Harmful chemicals when interacting with food (especially hot/ warm stuff) pass harmful effects to our body. For example, plastic water bottles (with inferior quality) contain many chemicals that are bisphenol A, or BPA, and phthalates, among others. These chemicals present in the container leach into bottled water when the usage of the bottles is prolonged. It is also seen that many individuals still use plastic water bottles for storing water for their day-to-day use that are supposed to be used only for once. Different types of plastic material show the chemicals used in that material and it is indicated inside the triangle of arrows on the bottom of the product/bottle. Studies on a number of natural resource bodies have already pointed out the harmful effects of prolonged use of plastics (especially of old and inferior-quality products).

More than that, the worry part here is that these plastic containers or bottles after the usage are not disposed of adequately. Discarded items are often dumped in landfills, or are floating on rivers, oceans and sidewalks. It is estimated that there are approximately 46,000 pieces of plastic floating on the sea per square mile. This has a number of harmful effects, harmful chemicals are leaked into the water bodies and also kill lots of the creatures inhabiting there, thus disrupting the whole ecosystem. It is also studied that some toxins that are leaked even can be a cause of cancer and reproductive disabilities. Unfortunately, only recycling can be the option and solution for this, which is only 12 per cent (as per estimate for the USA) out of the 35 billion bottles used in one year.

Saving Matters: Calculate Saving in Money and Resource Angle

Here is the example of a homemaker. The example is simple on understanding 'ways of performing our duties with an eye on environment'.

Sunita (name changed) is a homemaker. She is a graduate in biology and has two children, aged 10 and 5. She is leading a happy and satisfied life. She is an aware citizen and knows her duties related to environment conservation. She follows the principle of reducing the usage of resources so that one can contribute towards the bigger goal of environment and safety. Some of the practices what she follows are as follows.

She uses Reverse Osmosis (RO) system for water purification at home. The RO cleans water, and in the process of getting 1 litre of purified water, approximately 1.5 litres of water is wasted. Sunita restores the water thrown out from RO waste outlet in the process of cleaning. She uses that water for cleaning utensils and washing clothes. For the ease of storing water and reusing it, she has fixed a tank near the RO waste outlet. In a day with this process she reuses approximately 20 litres of water. Another practice followed by her is that she never serves full glass of water to anyone. If we calculate per day water saving capacity of a family, it is almost 3–4 litres of water. Another practice she follows is that she washes utensils only once a day. As per her theory, if we wash utensils three times a day versus one time a day, we are saving more than half amount of water used for cleaning utensils. Thus, Sunita saves per day approximately 10–15 litres of water in this way.

Another change she had made is in the layout and placing the furniture in her home. She has placed the study table near the window. While working her family does not need artificial light as one can very well study or do any other work with the help of natural light. Another habit is switching off lights and fans when are not in use. More dependence on fans and using AC only when it is necessary impact positively on the health as well.

One more intervention in the day-to-day life is cooking food half an hour before actual consumption. This reduces the need of reheating. As we all know that food needs to be eaten within half an hour of cooking for getting the best results from it. It does not require reheating. This saves energy and ultimately her house energy bill.

Capitalizing on Passion

The story is an example of how passion can be converted into a profession even without planning in that direction.

Sunaina and Ridhima used to work for an NGO in a place near Delhi. The NGO was working for children below poverty line. These children were generally those who were abandoned by their families. The NGO was taking care of their education and basic needs to fulfil their necessities by providing them some work. Initially, these children were trained on skills such as baking and making jewellery of pearls, metals and thread. When the children learnt the basic skill sets, they were employed by some other NGOs associated with such works of manufacturing and selling.

These NGOs have a good network and they organize fairs and exhibitions regularly to sell their products.

One day when Sunaina and Ridhima visited a house to deliver the order of jewellery manufactured by their NGO, they noticed that the homemaker was collecting garbage in two different pots. One pot was of green colour which was used for collecting trash of vegetables and fruits (biodegradable) and the other pot of red colour was used for collecting waste such as broken pieces of glass and empty tins. At the same time a garbage vehicle came to collect the garbage and the garbage was given by their house help to the garbage collector. At that time, both the girls were outside the house and they saw that the garbage collector had taken the garbage. They were curious, thus, they asked the driver of the vehicle as what they do of these two different garbage. But to their surprise, the driver said, what is the use of collecting all the garbage in two different packets when at the end both are going to get mixed. This was really shocking for both of them. They themselves saw that the household had put lots of efforts to collect the biodegradable and non-biodegradable waste in two different bins and this was taken care of by the garbage vehicle as well. But the end was not as per their expectations when all the efforts of the supply chain had gone in vain. They shared the incident with the founder of their NGO. The NGO took the initiative to influence and talk to the people and officers involved in the complete supply chain. These efforts paid them off and now the garbage is not getting mixed at the end and the small efforts of each household are actually giving benefits to many.

Environment Crusader at Home

Mihika had led a very carefree life until she became friend with Anushka. Anushka worked for an NGO in the EM domain. Anushka's repeated conversations on the importance of environment and an individual's role in EM changed Mihika's approach to living life. Now, she was actively scouting around the house trying to reduce wastage of resources and increase use of biodegradable stuff. She stopped all forms of paper billing and subscription to hardcopies of magazines and newspapers. She made some rules for all the members in the family—nobody was supposed to leave a room without switching off all the lights and electronic devices, the AC temperatures were not to be lowered too much as it leads to excessive consumption of energy along with that throwing of waste in separate bins designated for wet and dry waste. Initially, the family did not take these changes well but over a period of time with repeated badgering from Mihika, the family began acting responsibly. Mihika made changes in the kitchen also. She banished all the plastic and replaced the plastic containers with glass/metal ones. She made small changes to save cooking gas and used the kitchen waste-water for watering her garden and made compost from kitchen waste for nurturing the plants. Mihika also began attending Anushka's environmental awareness workshops and shared her tips on practising sustainability at home.

To sum up here, the benefits to both organization and employees are listed as follows:

For Organization

- Cost reduction

- Improved efficiency

- Better compliance on sustainability

- Increased trust and loyalty from employees

- Better retention

- Better image of the company

- Customers' support and loyalty

- Improved credibility of the company

- Enhanced market share and growth

- Societal support

For Employees

- Opportunity to contribute for a real cause

- Prospects to learn and grow

- Opportunity to mark oneself

- Better satisfaction

- Saving of resources at home as well because of improved habits towards conservation

- Chance to meet and work with people from other departments and a different level

- The opportunity to use practices learnt at work at home and saving money on personal bills

- The chance to involve in an issue that they are really concerned about

'There is no real ending. It's just the place where you stop the story.'

— Frank Herbert

There is a lot that can be done even in our homes. Why not to start today, contributing a bit. A Hindi proverb says: *Boond boond se bharta sagar.*

The small steps can reduce the landfill waste, clean the air and preserve the natural landscape. But here the need is to double our efforts. We can start with our homes, can teach our kids, institutionalize it in our institutions and so on. Some of the ideas and tips that can be easily implemented by all of us without tampering our busy daily schedule are as follows.

Beyond Organization: Key Takeaways

Some of the practices towards conserving natural resources are applied for commercial buildings can be replicated here in residential apartments as well. For example, the Raintree Hotel, Chennai, has used a material that is medium density fibre, bamboo and rubber wood. Some percentage of fly ash was mixed in cement at the time of construction. George Fisher concealed cistern, which uses one third of water from traditional system was also applied. RWH system and solar panels are one more addition in this direction.

Grow Your Own Food

If we have some space in our backyard, we can convert it into a beautiful kitchen garden for growing food for our daily usage. Let not be too ambitious initially, rather we can start with few handy vegetables and fruits. Growing vegetables and consuming them gives a lot of satisfaction to our body and mind. It has multiple positive results. Moreover, we are able to get fresh organic food available all the time without depending on anyone. In case we do not have space in the ground, or we are not staying in the ground floor, one can use the space available for balcony. Now the new designer concept of homes is facilitating in this direction where one can grow fruits and vegetable either on limited ground space or balcony or on the roof with some additional changes. We can also create homemade compost with the organic waste generated each day (almost 60 per cent of the total waste of home). Thus, we can remain modern with some thought in this direction and little effort with huge outcomes.

If one can look the case of a lower-middle income country like India in terms of waste creation, the story is not very different from the rich countries. An Indian family living in a city on an average produces 2.2 kg of waste each day. In a metro city, it is even more. But the surprising part is, out of the waste almost 60 per cent is made of organic material (kitchen waste) that includes peels of vegetables, fruits, unused grains or unused or rotten food. In most of the cases, all the waste whether organic or other is mixed and results in great difficulty in separating the waste for proper recycling.

'It is definitely easier to throw the waste out. But if you can convert it to useful and fertile "stench-free" compost without much hassle, why not?' That was the statement made by Ms Poonam Bir Kasturi, who had developed a habit of home composting.

Minimize Disposable/Non-disposable

Another routine can be in the direction of minimizing the use of disposable bags, especially made of plastic. Although, plastic is an easy source of keeping and carrying stuff in today's hectic daily schedule but if we can start a habit of carrying reusable bag to the market and keeping all the time folding cotton bags in our office bags or cars, we can at least minimize the use of disposable/non-disposable bags by 80–90 per cent.

When we are out of room or house, we can switch off lights and fans. This is just a change of habit and does not need much efforts. We can also replace the fuse bulbs and tube lights with LED ones at the time of purchasing new ones. We can also make a conscious choice of making a new electronic appliance, which claims that the electricity bill will get reduced because of the advanced technology. We can even buy gadgets with smart technology using sensor so that when someone is not present, they can remotely manage those appliances. All these conscious efforts will not only reduce the electricity consumption of the home but also at the end of the day one is contributing towards efforts to sustainability.

Looking Back to Our Traditions

One more tip in this direction is going back to our traditions. In India if we look back, we will find practices in homes of reusing old stuff. For example, old and faded towels are converted into dusters used for cleaning kitchen and floors. Old cloth sheets are reused for making beautiful table napkins. Instead of buying paper napkins, cloth napkins can be used and reused after washing them. Old curtains are converted into footrests. Old dresses can be designed into a new one considering the latest trend. Old coffee mugs can be converted into designer stationary holders. Empty glass jars are used for planting bonsais in homes. Empty jars of food like honey are collected and when having good number of jars available of same size, then after removing the earlier labels, new labels can be pasted and can be used for storing different food items. Scrap paper can be reused for different other purposes. Unused pages from kids' stationary can be collected and designed as a new writing pad.

Thus, the message here is loud and clear, traditionally, we believed in reusing and reducing the resources. This is the time that we follow our tradition with a way that looks trendy and ultimately reduces our expenditure. This is the time to look into ourselves and try to think creatively to make the bigger aim of sustainability a reality. A picture is worth a thousand words!

Watch Your Speed

We all understand that with limiting our speed of vehicle we can not only save fuel but also save ourselves with accidents, etc. We can switch off the engine of our vehicle if waiting on red light for more than 20–30 seconds. We can keep checking the condition of vehicle regularly. All these small interventions help in improving the durability of the engine and the surroundings.

In addition to this, we can also develop a habit of using staircases and taking walk when going to nearer distance. A lot of benefits from health to energy saving can be counted.

Go Digital

Why not educate ourselves and others about the benefits and ease of digital working? We can opt for 'green option' when visiting ATMs, in which paper slips are not generated after a transaction rather a message is received in our mobile, thus we can save lots of paper. Why to unnecessarily store lots of paper when we have gadgets in hand all the time.

Value Nature

We can start the effort with our place of living or society for having a provision of collecting rainwater which can be used further for watering the plants, etc. We can also make a provision of solar energy in our home or society. This is an initial step towards self-sustenance by lessening the burden on the planet.

Go Local

We can support the local community by buying local products or directly procuring them from the farmer in case of bulk purchase. Again, the savings are huge, and hassles will be less with reduced intermediaries.

Post Your Story

We can be creative and innovative. We can do a lot with less. Why not take a step and make a mission? Post your story with a contemporary outlook in your network, be it social media or blog or any other forum.

A journey just begun...

SUGGESTED READINGS

Global Reporting Initiative. (2015). *Sustainability and reporting trends in 2025: Preparing for the future.* Author.

Herrmann, C., Schmidt, C., Kurle, D., Blume, S., & Thiede, S. (2014). Sustainability in manufacturing and factories of the future. *International Journal of Precision Engineering and Manufacturing Green Technology, 1*(4), 283–292.

Pandey, P. C. (2020). Circular designing and green growth: Insights on future of sustainability. *Vision, 24*(1), 113–117. https://doi.org/10.1177/0972262920903904

https://indiacsr.in/sustainability-extended-producerresponsibility-policy-of-dell-in-india/

https://www.un.org/sustainabledevelopment/sustainable development-goals/

https://global.toyota/en/sustainability/esg/challenge2050/

https://www.law360.com/articles/624183/emerging-trends-in-corporate-sustainability-reporting

https://work.chron.com/ways-encourage-employees-green-4470.html

https://nbs.net/p/engaging-employees-in-going-green-b12b68c1-bc1e-4e14-a9b9-a31e14297361

https://www.greenhotelier.org/our-themes/community-communication-engagement/engaging-employees/

https://e-csr.net/definitions/green-human-resources-management-meaning-definition/

https://www.greenimpact.com/best-practices-and-tools/employee-engagementsustainabilitymake-green-happen/

https://work.chron.com/ways-encourage-employees-green-4470.html

https://nbs.net/p/engaging-employees-in-going-green-b12b68c1-bc1e-4e14-a9b9-a31e14297361

https://www.greenhotelier.org/our-themes/community-communication-engagement/engaging-employees/

https://e-csr.net/definitions/green-human-resources-management-meaning-definition/

https://www.greenimpact.com/best-practices-and-tools/employee-engagementsustainabilitymake-green-happen/

https://www.scholastic.com/teachers/blog-posts/beth-newingham/my-april-top-ten-list-going-green-at-school/

https://theartofsimple.net/tips-to-go-green-at-home/

https://www.cemnet.com/News/story/160966/india-s-central-pollution-control-board-issues-waste-guidelines.html

https://www.livestrong.com/article/183101-the-negative-effects-of-using-plastic-drinking-bottles/

http://www.gogreen.org/blog/impacts-of-plastic-water-bottles

https://yourstory.com/2019/07/eco-friendly-products-plastic-startups

https://yourstory.com/socialstory/2019/06/startup-ahmedabad-ecoright-plastic-alternatives-bag-disney

https://yourstory.com/2020/03/daily-dump-home-composter-waste-management

https://wedocs.unep.org/bitstream/handle/20.500.11822/25496/singleUsePlastic_sustainability.pdf

https://www.indiatoday.in/education-today/gk-current-affairs/story/green-initiative-268079-2015-10-14

GLOSSARY

Alternative fuel and raw material: This is an alternative source of fuel made up of waste such as oils, plastics, wood and tyres.

Bureau of Energy Efficiency: This programme is for energy audit and examination.

Business responsibility report: It is expected from the top listed companies to disclose the responsible practices to all stakeholders.

Circular economy: A circular economy is an economic system aimed at reducing waste and encouraging the reuse of resources.

Clean development mechanism: These are projects to reduce emissions.

Climate Disclosure Leadership Index: It recognizes companies with regular self-disclosure, sustainable governance and leadership to address issues related to climate change.

Climate risk: This is an assessment of the impact of climate change on business.

Closed-loop business model: It comprises products and business processes sketched in such a manner that enable waste into a new transformed substance.

Committee for Development Policy: This is a subsidiary body of the Economic and Social Council and the role of the committee is to suggest on issues related to the SDGs of 2030.

Corporate social responsibility: This is the process of becoming self-regulated and giving back to society with some efforts regularly to this direction.

Cradle-to-cradle: This is a closed-loop technical nutrient cycle with a biological open-loop cycle.

Delivering functionality: It believes that, rather than having ownership of all resources, services are hired that satisfy users' needs without owning physical products.

Downstream stewardship: It comprises proactively tackling health issues of consumers.

Economic performance: It is a company's annual financial performance report and covers various parameters.

Effluent treatment plant: Through this, the process of recycling water takes place.

Electro-deposition paint coating: It operates at low voltage and consumes less energy in paint operations.

Employee activism: Under this, employees take action against their employers for some controversial actions that can adversely affect society.

Environment management system: EMS integrates policies, process and practices by training, monitoring and evaluating environmental performance.

Environment, health and safety: Policy provides the necessary guidance towards the conservation of the environment.

Environment, society and governance: Criteria are set for examining the relationship of companies' performance as a steward of nature and society.

Environmental impact assessment: This tries to assess and estimate the total impact on the environment of certain policies, programmes, practices and further actions of the organization.

Environment management: This is followed by organizations to comply with environmental and sustainability norms.

Extended producer's responsibility: Under this, major responsibility is expected from the producer for treatment of the disposal of consumer products after their usage.

Fibre reinforced plastic: Under this, aerodynamic energy-efficient blades are replaced with standard blades at cooling towers for lower energy consumption.

Forest Stewardship Council: It helps in managing the forest body of the world in a responsible manner.

Fossil fuel substitutes: These are the ways of providing cleaner combustible substitutes for traditional liquid automobile fuels.

Frugal business model: It concentrates on the provision of products and services to low-income markets, often in extreme poverty.

Global Reporting Initiative: It is an independent body that helps organizations, government and non-governmental bodies in assessing issues related to the environment.

Green human resource management: It is the way of developing policies and practices in an organization that helps in building green behaviour of employees.

Green innovation: It consists of new or modified processes, practices, systems and products that benefit the environment and contribute to environmental sustainability.

Green Procurement Guidelines: The Green Procurement Guidelines are based on EU's end-of-life vehicle standards for auto parts. These guidelines are referred to for the recycling of auto parts in an eco-friendly manner at the end of their life cycle.

Green STAY: It is an initiative from Hotel Marriott. Green STAY helps in reforestation efforts.

Heating, ventilating, air-conditioning: It is a process in which the indoor air quality is maintained comfortably by proper ventilation and filtration.

Hydroponic greenhouse: This is a substitute for production where plants are grown in a nutrient solution with adequate heat and ventilation.

Industrial symbiosis: This is a process adaptation solution that turns waste products from one process into feedstock for another process or product line.

Industry Inc: It is a group of companies engaged in similar businesses, such as manufacturing steel and providing telecom services.

International Union for Conservation of Nature: Under this, the conservation of nature is promoted, along with doing analysis and research for better education and training.

Investment risk: It is the uncertainty of receiving returns on investments.

Investment stewardship: In this, one becomes a custodian of and makes investment on behalf of investors.

Kaizen and quality circles: It is a philosophy pioneered in Japan and is based on continuous improvement for making an efficient system while reducing the wastage of time.

Key result area: It refers to the goals and parameters set for an employee for a specific role and time.

KSA: It refers to the knowledge, skills and abilities of individuals.

Leadership in Energy and Environment Design: It provides a framework for designing green buildings that are highly efficient, healthy and cost saving as well.

Lean Manufacturing: It identifies and pertains to lessen waste in production processes.

Mission LAUNCH: LAUNCH tries to assess and solve global issues related to water, health, energy, waste and systems.

Mission statement: A document that explains the reason why an organization exists and what kind of activities it can be engaged in.

National Mission for Green India: A green initiative under the Ministry of Environment, which approves four states, and is an important thrust to the great cause.

Nationally Determined Contributions: These create awareness and educate on issues related to GHG.

Natural Capitalism: This is a radical transformation in energy efficiency and material productivity.

Natural Resources Defense Council: This aims to protect natural resources.

New Economy Concepts (e.g., Blue Economy): In line with the concept of green economy, 'blue economy' encourages better stewardship of natural resources, that is, oceans, river bodies, etc.

Organisation for Economic Co-operation and Development: The OECD forum is committed to providing a platform for seeking solutions to common issues and problems that occur while working in a global scenario.

Perform, achieve, trade: This is a way towards energy saving based on energy-saving targets for improving energy efficiency.

Portfolio construction: This means investing in a variety of funds that will give good returns.

Price product service: This is a system based on paying for service per work.

Sewage treatment plant: In this, physical, chemical and biological processes are used to remove harmful contaminants for treating household sewage and industrial wastewater.

Social impact assessment: It is the process of assessing policies and practices to see the impact on society and the consequences.

Solar reflective: It is a kind of material that keeps the surface cool by reflecting solar radiation and emitting thermal radiation.

Stewardship role: It means to actively engage with all stakeholders to ensure their long-term health and well-being.

Strategic business model: A business model that creates competitive advantage through superior customer value.

Supply chain partners: The vendors who provide raw material and ingredients to organizations.

Sustainable Development Goals: These are a collection of 17 global goals set by the UN General Assembly.

Thermal substitution rate: This is the calculation of the proportionate substitute of traditional fossil fuels using alternative fuels.

Total injury frequency rate: This is the calculation of time based on the number of fatalities, and the lost time due to injuries needs to be substituted by others.

Trade Union Sustainable Development Advisory Committee: Its purpose is to strengthen the capacity of workers and trade unions for supporting sustainable development.

Triple bottom line: It can be defined as getting an improvement in performance based on economic, environmental and social activities.

Triple E: It basically involves economics, the environment and equity.

Trust quotient: The degree to which the organization is trusted by customers and other stakeholders.

WEarth: Under this hotel, guests plant a tree for each night they stay at the Hotel Marriott. The WEarth initiative plants actual trees on behalf of guests.

Zero emissions: It means no discharge of carbon dioxide and other gaseous substances that pollute the environment.

ABOUT THE AUTHORS

Dr Soni Agrawal holds a doctorate in Management from the Indian Institute of Technology Kharagpur. She has a blend of experience in both industry and academia. She has trained senior and mid-level executives in the areas of HR analytics, PM, motivation and attitude building. Some of the companies included in the list are CESC, PCBL, Oxford University Press, India Post, LIC, etc. Prior to joining academics, she worked for industry in the area of strategy and human resource development. As a researcher, she published research papers in reputed national and international journals and reviewed a number of books and manuscripts. She also chaired sessions in various seminars/conferences.

Dr Roma Puri is an Associate Professor and teaches organizational behaviour and HRM in IMI Kolkata and has a PhD from the Indian Institute of Management Calcutta. Dr Roma Puri has more than a decade of teaching experience. Her domain has been organizational behaviour and HRM. She has taught courses at graduate and post-graduate level. In addition to teaching regular courses at B-schools, she has also taught HRM-related courses in the Career Oriented Programme offered by St. Xavier's College. With a keen interest in behavioural sciences, she has gone received intensive group process training from the Indian Society for Applied Behavioural Science, attended the Group Relations Conference and offered several pro-grammes in this area. She has been a part of the Global Leadership and Organizational Behaviour Effectiveness (GLOBE) programme led by Professor Robert House at the Wharton School.